The Developing Child

Recent decades have witnessed unprecedented advances in research on human development. Each book in The Developing Child series reflects the importance of this research as a resource for enhancing children's well-being. It is the purpose of the series to make this resource available to that increasingly large number of people who are responsible for raising a new generation. We hope that these books will provide rich and useful information for parents, educators, child-care professionals, students of developmental psychology, and all others concerned with childhood.

Jerome Bruner, New School for Social Research
Michael Cole, University of California, San Diego
Barbara Lloyd, University of Sussex
Series Editors

The Developing Child Series

The First Relationship

Mother and Infant

Daniel Stern

Harvard University Press
Cambridge, Massachusetts

Library of Congress Cataloging in Publication Data
Stern, Daniel, 1934-
    The first relationship.

    (The Developing child)
    Bibliography: p.
    Includes index.
    1. Infant psychology. 2. Parent and child.
3. Interpersonal communication. 4. Social inter-
action. I. Title. II. Series.
BF723.I6S66   155.4'22   77-6763
ISBN 0-674-30431-4
ISBN 0-674-30432-2 pbk.

For my children
Michael, Maria, Kaia

Acknowledgments

The writing of this book owes much to discussion with a number of colleagues and co-workers, and to the suggestions and criticisms they offered. In most cases their contribution relates not only to the writing of the book but also to the years of research and exchange of ideas that it is based on. I would like to mention especially Joseph Jaffe, Beatrice Beebe, Gail A. Wasserman, Stephen Bennett, Sam Anderson, John Gibbon, J. Craig Peery, and Liz Sharpless. I would also like to acknowledge Lawrence C. Kolb and Howard F. Hunt who, in addition to being invaluable mentors, were crucially instrumental in my pursuit of these studies. Much of the research was supported by the William T. Grant Foundation; The Research Foundation for Mental Hygiene, New York State; and The Jane Hilder Harris Foundation. I am especially indebted to Phyllis Jacobs for help with the preparation of the manuscript, and to Susan W. Baker for the unflagging encouragement she has given in the writing of this book. Most of all I want to pay tribute to the parents who have let us learn from them at first hand.

D.S.

Contents

Credits

The First Relationship

1 / Learning about Things Human

We have watched social interactions between caregivers and infants in their homes, in the laboratory, on playgrounds, in parks, on subways, anywhere. The purpose of this search has been to understand how, in the short span of the first six months of life, the infant emerges as a social human being. Somehow, in this brief period that I shall call the first phase of learning about things human, the baby will have learned how to invite his mother to play and then initiate an interaction with her;* he will have become expert at maintaining and modulating the flow of a social exchange; he will have acquired the signals to terminate or avoid an interpersonal encounter, or just place it temporarily in a "holding pattern." In general, he will have mastered most of the basic signals and conventions so that he can perform the "moves" and run off patterned sequences in step with those of his mother, resulting in the dances that we recognize as social interactions. This biologically designed choreography will serve as a prototype for all his later interpersonal exchanges.

This book is about what I have learned of the early social interactive process: the behavior of both caregiver and infant that go into its making, its structure, goals, and developmental functions. This is not a how-to book, but rather a what-is book.

My guiding notion in conducting this search has been simple. The caregiver and infant, whether they are aware of it or not, "know" more than we do about their own social interactions.

*I shall designate all infants by male pronouns and all caregivers by female pronouns. I hope that the disadvantages of this convention will be outweighed by the advantages of easier and clearer reading.

They alone, acting and interacting as they normally do, had to be my teachers. The mother is involved in a natural process with her baby, a process that unfolds with a fascinating intricacy and complexity for which both she and the baby are well prepared by millennia of evolution. Since they "know intuitively" how their own exchanges work and feel, I had to find out how best to learn from them things that do not necessarily lend themselves to telling or explaining in words. To do this, my colleagues and I sometimes were simply observers, taking in with our eyes and ears interactive events as they occurred. These events, however, go by very quickly and only once. To cope with this problem, we sometimes videotaped regularly in the participants' homes. We could then view and review the tapes many times over, back in our laboratory. When we felt that even finer-grained observations were needed, we studied 16 millimeter films frame by frame, spending hours examining events that occur in seconds. At other times, we recorded certain selected behaviors, such as gazing or vocalizing, and fed the records into a computer to help us look for patterns and relationships.

Before proceeding further, I want to describe the kind of events we focused on and learned from. They are the fairly ordinary and common interpersonal exchanges occurring between a primary caregiver and an infant during the first half year of life. These are moments that are almost purely social in nature. They often occur at unlikely or unexpected times in the middle of or in the space between other activities. Yet, as I shall try to show, these interpersonal moments are crucial in forming the experiences from which the infant learns how to relate to other people. Here is a detailed example that gives the flavor of the phenomenon and will serve as a reference later on.

A mother is bottle feeding her three-and-a-half-month-old boy. They are about halfway through. During the first half of the feeding the baby had been sucking away, working seriously and occasionally looking at his mother, sometimes for long stretches (10 to 15 seconds). At other times he gazed lazily around the room. Mother had been fairly still. She glanced at her baby periodically, sort of checking, and every now and then looked at him with a good long look (20-30 seconds) but without talking to him or changing the expression on her face. She rarely said anything when she looked at him, but when she looked away toward me she often talked, and with much facial animation.

Until this point, a normal feeding, not a social interaction, was underway. Then a change began. While talking and looking at me the mother turned her head and gazed at the infant's face. He was gazing at the ceiling, but out of the corner of his eye he saw her head turn toward him and turned to gaze back at her. This had happened before, but now he broke rhythm and stopped sucking. He let go of the nipple and the suction around it broke as he eased into the faintest suggestion of a smile. The mother abruptly stopped talking and, as she watched his face begin to transform, her eyes opened a little wider and her eyebrows raised a bit. His eyes locked on to hers, and together they held motionless for an instant. The infant did not return to sucking and his mother held frozen her slight expression of anticipation. This silent and almost motionless instant continued to hang until the mother suddenly shattered it by saying "Hey!" and simultaneously opening her eyes wider, raising her eyebrows further, and throwing her head up and toward the infant. Almost simultaneously, the baby's eyes widened. His head tilted up and, as his smile broadened, the nipple fell out of his mouth. Now she said, "Well hello!...heelló...heeelloóoo!", so that her pitch rose and the "hellos" became longer and more stressed on each successive repetition. With each phrase the baby expressed more pleasure, and his body resonated almost like a balloon being pumped up, filling a little more with each breath. The mother then paused and her face relaxed. They watched each other expectantly for a moment. The shared excitement between them ebbed, but before it faded completely, the baby suddenly took an initiative and intervened to rescue it. His head lurched forward, his hands jerked up, and a fuller smile blossomed. His mother was jolted into motion. She moved forward, mouth open and eyes alight, and said, "Oooooh...ya wanna play do ya...yeah?...I didn't know if you were still hungry . . . no . . . nooooo . . . no I didn't . . . " And off they went.

After some easy exchange the pace and excitement increased to a higher level at which the interaction assumed the form of a repeating game. The cycles in the game went something like this. The mother moved closer, leaning in, frowning, but with a twinkle in her eyes and her mouth pursed in a circle always on the edge of breaking into a smile. She said, "This time I'm gonna get ya," simultaneously poising her hand over the baby's belly ready to begin a finger-tickle-march up the baby's belly and into the hilarious recesses of his neck and armpits. As she hovered and spoke, he smiled and squirmed but always stayed in eye contact with her. Even the actual tickle-march did not break their mutual gaze.

After the finger-march had reached the neck and was punctuated with a final tickle, the mother moved back and away rapidly in her chair. Her face opened up and her eyes wandered off as if she were thinking of a new and even more irresistible plan for her next approach. The baby emitted a just audible "aaah" as he watched, captivated, as she let her notions pass freely across her face, as if it were a transparent screen flashing the changing pictures in her mind.

Finally, she rushed forward again, perhaps a bit earlier and with more acceleration than the times before. His readiness had not fully settled yet, and he was caught a split second off guard. His face showed more surprise than pleasure. His eyes were wide and his mouth open but not turned up at the corners. He slightly averted his face but still held his end of the mutual gaze. When she moved back at the end of that cycle she saw that it had missed somehow—not quite backfired, but missed enough. The pleasure had disappeared. She sat back in her chair for several seconds, talking aloud to herself and to him but without doing anything, just evaluating. She then resumed the game. This time, however, she left out the tickle-march part and established a more regular and marked cadence in her actions. She moved in, more evenly, with her eyebrows, eyes, and mouth in dramatic changing displays that promised, but with less threat, to do what she said, "I'm gonna get ya." The baby's attention was again riveted to her, and he began to show an easy smile with his mouth partly open, the face tilted up, and the eyes slightly closed.

During the next four cycles of the renewed and slightly varied game, the mother did pretty much the same, except that on each successive cycle she escalated the level of suspense with her face and voice and timing. It went something like: "I'm gonna get ya" . . . "I'mmm gonna get ya" . . . . I'mmmm gooonaa gétcha" . . . . . "I'mmmm gooooonaaa gétcha!!" The baby became progressively more aroused, and the mounting excitement of both of them contained elements of both glee and danger. During the first cycle the baby stayed captivated by his mother's antics. He smiled broadly and never took his eyes off her face. During the second cycle, he averted his face slightly as she approached, but the smile held. At the beginning of the third sortie by the mother, the baby had still not resumed the full face-to-face position and had his head turned slightly away. As she approached, his face turned even further but still he kept looking at her. At the same time, his smile flattened. The eyebrows and the corners of his mouth flickered back and forth between a smile and a sober expression. As the excitement mounted he seemed to run that narrow path between explosive glee and fright. As the path got narrower, he finally broke gaze with mother, appearing thereby to recompose himself for a second, to deescalate his own level of excitement. Having done so successfully, he returned his gaze to mother and exploded into a big grin. On that cue she began, with gusto, her fourth and most suspenseful cycle, but this one proved too much for him and pushed him across to the other side of the narrow path. He broke gaze immediately, turned away, face averted, and frowned. The mother picked it up immediately. She stopped the game dead in its tracks and said softly, "Oh honey, maybe you're still hungry, huh . . . let's try some milk again." He returned gaze. His face eased and he took the nipple again. The "moment" of social interaction was over. Feeding has resumed. (This whole episode lasted about four minutes.)

From the analysis of such "moments" we have learned that the purely social interactions, sometimes called "free play," between mother and infant are among the most crucial experiences in the infant's first phase of learning and participating in human events. By the end of the first six months the work of this phase is done, and it is considerable.

The infant has developed schemas of the human face, voice, and touch, and within those categories he knows the specific face, voice, touch, and movements of his primary caregiver. He has acquired schemas of the various changes they undergo to form different human emotional expressions and signals. He has "got" the temporal patterning of human behavior and the meaning of different changes and variations in tempo and rhythm. He has learned the social cues and conventions that are mutually effective in initiating, maintaining, terminating, and avoiding interactions with his mother. He has learned different discursive or dialogic modes, such as turn taking. And he now has the foundation of some internal composite picture of his mother so that, a few months after this phase is over, we can speak of his having established object permanence—or an enduring representation of mother that he carries around with him with or without her presence.

To understand how the developmental tasks of this first phase are accomplished I shall pursue the following plan. First I shall examine the repertoire of facial, vocal, and other behaviors that the average caregiver provides for the infant as his first and foremost experience with the world of human stimuli. Next I shall examine the repertoire of behaviors and perceptual abilities that the infant possesses to perceive and act with in the world of human behavior he finds himself in. I will then discuss some experimental findings and theoretical frameworks which help us understand how the mother's and the infant's separate behaviors might influence one another, and then how the interaction is actually structured, toward what goals, and to accomplish what developmental functions. Finally, in a more clinical chapter I shall discuss some ways in which the interaction can go awry.

2 / The Caregiver's Repertoire

The infant's first exposure to the human world consists simply of whatever his mother actually does with her face, voice, body, and hands. The ongoing flow of her acts provides for the infant his emerging experience with the stuff of human communication and relatedness. This choreography of maternal behaviors is the raw material from the outside world with which the infant begins to construct his knowledge and experience of all things human: the human presence; the human face and voice, their forms and changes that make up expressions; the units and meaning of human behaviors; the relationship between his own behavior and someone else's.

After a great deal of watching mothers and infants play, I gradually realized that I was overlooking an obvious but important fact. Mothers act very differently with infants than they do with other adults or older children. This fact is so common and expected that it had been taken for granted and generally gone unnoticed as a phenomenon of any scientific interest. Caregivers not only do different things in the presence of infants, but they perform them differently. "Baby talk" is the most obvious, and best studied, example, even though we are just beginning to understand its complexities. Baby talk, however, turns out to be only part of a much larger picture: almost all the forms of a mother's social behavior directed toward the baby are relatively specific to infants. The "faces" she makes for the infant, the way she uses her speech, not only what she says but the sounds she emits, the movements of her head and body, the things she does with her hands and fingers, how she positions herself in relation

9

to the infant, and the timing and rhythm of her behaviors; all of these become different when directed to an infant.

Compared to most acceptable and appropriate adult-to-adult social behaviors, the repertoire of a mother's actions toward her infant are quite unusual, in fact, highly deviant. They would be considered outright bizarre if performed toward anyone but an infant (with the partial exception of a young animal or perhaps a lover). When so directed, however, they comprise an expected and normal special subset of human behaviors, a subset belonging to the larger category of parental behaviors. I call this behavioral constellation "infant-elicited social behaviors."

With the obvious no longer taken for granted, many new questions emerge: what is the repertoire of this special subset and what are its characteristics; what is there about the baby that elicits these particular behaviors; who besides mothers do and can perform these behaviors; what functions, if any, may these behaviors serve for the infant's survival and development; are these behaviors specifically elicited by human infants alone; and how do they differ from culture to culture?

DESCRIPTION OF INFANT-ELICITED SOCIAL BEHAVIORS

A word of warning first. My point is *not* to describe these behaviors so that caregivers will perform them, or perform them "better." Caregivers usually perform them naturally, almost unawares. In fact, if you call a mother's attention to exactly what she is doing, she will say "Yes, of course, so?" I also have no intention of making a caregiver acutely conscious of every little movement and sound she makes. Each caregiver develops her own style of usage, fitted to who she is and who her baby is. Happily I'm sure there is nothing I can say that would interfere with that natural exchange.

There are, however, two compelling reasons to describe these behaviors: to indicate (and offer reassurance) that most of the "unusual" things a mother does are a normal and necessary aspect of that part of human biology we call parenting—actions to be enjoyed; and second, to characterize them so that we can imagine what they look, sound, and feel like from the infant's point of view.

Facial expressions. The facial expressions that caregivers make for infants are exaggerated in time and space. Two very common examples will suffice, the mock-surprise expression and the frown. When a mother is trying to get an infant's attention and he turns to look at her, the instant he does so, she is most likely to perform a mock-surprise expression. Her eyes open very wide, the eyebrows go up, the mouth opens wide, and the head is raised and tilted up slightly. At the same time, she usually says something like "oooooh" or "aaaaah." This expression is fairly stereotyped but has innumerable minor variations: the mouth may form a smile, or form a large circle with or without pursed lips or even stay closed; the head may move toward the baby rather than up and back, or it may tilt to one side; and of course the entire fullness of display may vary from a mild displacement of facial parts in space to a full-blown facial display where each part is displaced to its maximal position—that is, eyes as wide open as possible, eyebrows as high as possible, and so on.

So far we have looked at only exaggeration in space, in the degree of fullness of the display. There is also an exaggeration in time, in duration of the performance of the display. Compared to adult-to-adult social expressions, these facial displays are generally slow to form and are then held for a long time. Take one good example of a full display of a mock-surprise expression. Generally, the expression grows slowly almost as if the mother were performing in slow motion, gradually but dramatically building to the fullest degree of the display and then, once "there," holding the achieved position for an extremely long time (relatively speaking). At other times, mothers speed up their behaviors in an exaggerated way, and at other times they "play" with the speed and rate of behavior flow, varying it with changes of pace and unexpected spurts and runs.

The second common example is the frown. Here the main features are the progressive knitting and lowering of eyebrows, with the consequent narrowing of the eyes. Typically the head averts to the side and slightly down, the mouth forms a small circle or it purses, and the wings of the nose tense (in a fuller display there may be nose wrinkling). There is often a vocalization "aaaaooooh" with a sliding drop in pitch and a decrescendo in volume toward the end. At its fullest the expression looks something like disgust. Here too, as with the mock surprise, the exaggeration is such that a still shot of these expressions often looks like a caricature or very bad acting. Smiles, pouts, lip pursings, and their many variations conform to the same modes of performance.

There are three other facial expressions of particular importance in the repertoire of infant-elicited facial expressions: the smile, which needs no description; the "Oh, you poor dear" expression of concern and sympathy, which combines elements of the mock-surprise expression and the frown, in that the brows are slightly knit but the eyes are widened, the mouth is usually partly opened and the head is tilted or aligned in the same plane as the infant's and comes toward the infant's; the last "expression," a neutral or expressionless face, is hardly unique to but quite important in the infant-elicited situation. Each of the five expressions are common, ubiquitous, and performed very frequently and stereotypically during play interactions. They have been singled out here because of their special signal value in regulating the course of early interactions between caregivers and infants.

During her interactions with her infant a mother rarely, if ever, needs or uses the full range of human expressions available to her. Only a limited set of expressions is needed at this point in development to regulate the most general flow of the interaction, and to mark major nodal points in that flow. The most bareboned set of signals for this purpose would consist of displays to initiate, to maintain and modulate, to terminate, and to avoid a social interaction.

(1) To initiate or signal a readiness or invitation to interaction: The mock-surprise expression serves this function. It looks like a caricature of an orienting or surprise response and has much in common with the universal facial greeting behaviors described by Eibl-Eibesfeldt and by Kendon and Ferber.[1] In some types of play interactions it is the most common expression seen. It may occur every 10 to 15 seconds—almost every time the infant refocuses his visual attention on the mother. It is as if she is regreeting him each time and redisplaying her orientation to him as a signal to indicate readiness for a potential interaction as well as to stimulate it.

(2) The maintenance and modulation of an ongoing interaction: The smile and the expression of concern serve these func-

tions. The smile is a potent affirmative signal that the interaction is not only ongoing but going well. The concern expression is also seen when the interaction is ongoing but when it is running down or into trouble. It is a clear attempt, and perhaps a signal of the mother's intent, to refocus, reengage, and thereby maintain the interaction.

(3) The termination of the interaction: The frown with head aversion and breaking of gaze is a signal to stop, at least for the moment, an interaction that is no longer working for the baby or the mother or both. The termination can, of course, be momentary and followed by the signal to reinitiate the interaction by starting again differently.

(4) The avoidance of a social interaction: A neutral or expressionless face, especially with gaze aversion, is a clear signal of the nonreadiness or lack of intent to interact.

All the "basic" emotional facial displays, such as fear, anger, joy, surprise, disgust, consist of constellations that are made from different combinations of the separate movements or positions of each of the facial parts: eyes, mouth, eyebrows, and so on. Across all cultures we recognize these constellations as largely innate. In addition to each constellation, which corresponds to a basic emotion, having an innate signal value, certain movements of separate facial parts, even dissociated from known constellations, may also have innate signal properties. For instance, in emotional displays where the eyes are widened (generally with eyebrow raising or flashing, to indicate surprise, awe, flirting, greeting), the common feature of the signal is its indication of readiness to interact and a heightened focus of attention on the other. Conversely, when the eyes are narrowed (and the eyebrows are knitted or lowered) as in anger, fear, disapproval, or disgust, the common signal feature is the probable intention of reduced readiness to interact and the potential of attenuating or breaking of attentional focus. In a similar fashion moving the head up or toward the other or aligning it in the same plane accompany positive interaction-maintaining displays; moving the head down, back, or especially away to the side generally indicates the reverse, an intent to terminate. Wide opening of the mouth is positive and interaction-maintaining while mouth narrowing does the opposite. In this manner the maternal infant-elicited facial displays provide signals indicating a state of general readiness and intent regarding the very existence of an interaction as well as providing experience with some of the common basic features of what may also be specific emotional expressions for the infant.

The mother in the major facial displays she performs for the infant exaggerates in particular those elements (eye widening or narrowing, eyebrow raising or knitting, and such) that serve as strong signals relating to the intention to start, maintain, terminate, or avoid a focused interaction. The other signal features of the mother's expression may initially be lost to the infant or irrelevant to him.

Infant-elicited social behaviors appear to have three salient characteristics. They are exaggerated in space and the fullness of display can be maximal. Their performance is exaggerated in time, usually marked by a slow formation and an elongated duration. And the repertoire is usually limited to several selected expressions that are performed very frequently and with much stereotypy. These performance features of the mother's facial behavior no doubt facilitate the infant's ability to learn human facial expressions. The spatial and temporal exaggeration coupled with the frequent and stereotyped performance of only selected displays would throw those behaviors into high relief and greatly aid the infant in disembedding them from the "background" movements of other expressions which may be less crucial at this point in development, or from movements that "simply" accompany speech. As we shall see, the same three characteristics of infant-elicited social behaviors in other modalities, such as vocalization, may serve the same function there too, of presenting salient human behaviors so that their recognition and discrimination will be readily enhanced.

Vocalization. Speech is conveniently divided into what is said (content) and the way it is said (prosodic features). Ferguson, in a fascinating paper entitled "Baby Talk in Six Languages,"[2] studied what mothers said to their infants in six diverse languages from different continents. He found that they all spoke their version of baby talk to infants. In each case there was very simplified syntax, short length of utterance; many nonsense sounds; and certain transformations of sounds which had some common features in all languages. For example, mothers around the globe would perform their languages' counterpart of transforming "pretty rabbit" to "pwitty wabbit."

Many other researchers, notably Nelson and Bloom, have examined how a mother teaching an older (two years) infant to speak will automatically use fewer words in a sentence and keep the syntax simple.[3] Then progressively over the following months the mother will make her sentences longer and more complex as the child "gets it," keeping in step with the child's growing language skills but still always staying a step or two ahead of the child.

What is more striking, however, when one listens to a caregiver speak to a younger infant of a few months of age, is *how* the mother talks rather than what she says.[4] First of all, the pitch of the voice is almost invariably raised. It is common to hear a mother (or father) run off long stretches of speech in a falsetto range. Many of these falsetto runs will be perfectly good English sentences; others may consist of squeaks and squeals mixed in with some words. At other times, to the infant's delight, the caregiver will switch, sometimes suddenly, to a throaty false bass range. Once again, when "fooling around" in the bass range the mixture of words and animal type sounds can be marvelously diverse.

Of more importance is the point made earlier about facial expressions. The caregiver exaggerates the range of her behavior—in this case, vocal pitch. It is as if she were preparing the infant with adequate experience and exposure to any and all types of salient sounds that other humans are likely to emit. The loudness or intensity of vocalizations is also exaggerated, spanning a range from a rich variety of whispered sounds to loud "pretend-scary" or exuberant exclamations. Changes in the intensity of sound are also varied more richly and dramatically than in normal adult speech. Similarly, there is a more pronounced stress placed on words or syllables. The different rhythms and syncopations that result contribute to the sing-song quality of much of infant-elicited maternal speech.

Beyond exaggerations in degree or extent of performance, the other general characteristic of infant-elicited speech is the altered speed of performance. Here, as in the case of facial expressions, the timing of events is sometimes exaggeratedly speeded up, but generally it is slowed down. Vowel duration is longer. This commonplace event can increase emphasis on certain words or phrases, as in "what a goooood little baby," or can be used simply to underscore the communicative or social rather than the linguistic event, as when a mother "comments" on an infant's facial expression by saying "aaaahooooooh." Similarly, the rate of change in pitch and loudness is also generally slower, frequently resulting in dramatic crescendos, decrescendos, or glissandos. Last, the pauses between each maternal utterance are elongated, allowing a longer time to process what was just said before the next communication arrives. This, however, is not necessarily why the mother makes her pauses longer. A mother-infant vocal dialogue is an unusual one. It is more a monologue by the mother in the form of an imaginary dialogue, for the reason that, although the infant rarely vocalizes back, the mother generally behaves as if he had. Figure 1 illustrates this point. It shows the average duration of a vocalization and its subsequent pause in the following situations: (1) an adult dialogue; (2) maternal vocalizations to an infant; (3) infant vocalizations to a mother; and (4) a combination of elements of 1, 2, and 3.[5] Why when vocalizing to an infant does the mother shorten her utterance and elongate her pause? One plausible explanation for the longer pause is that after speaking the mother waits the average

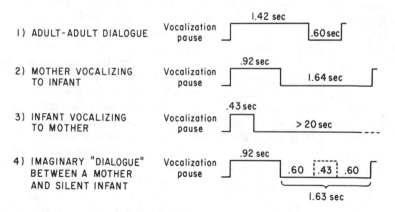

1. *The average duration of a vocalization and its subsequent pause in four different dialogic situations.*

adult dialogue pause length (.60 second). She then remains silent for the duration of an imagined infant vocal response (.43 second) and then again waits the average adult dialogue pause length (.60 second) before speaking again. If we assume this, then we get the timing shown in the imaginary dialogue (4). The three pauses combined (.60 + .43 + .60 seconds = 1.63 seconds) almost exactly equals the elongated pauses we see when mother is vocalizing to the infant (1.64), shown in line (2) of Figure 1. An example illustrates this situation easily:

Mother: "Aren't you my cutie?"   (1.42 seconds)
Pause: (.60 second)
Imagined response from infant: "Yes"   (.43 second)
Pause: (.60 second)
Mother: "You sure are."

This situation is partially the result of mothers' directing so many of their vocalizations to infants in the form of questions where an imagined response is easily simulated.

In any event, the infant is exposed to a vocal burst-pause temporal pattern from the mother which delivers shorter vocal "packages" to process; provides a longer period in which to process the package; and exposes him to the mature time frame to which his later dialogic skills must conform. In other words, he is being taught how to take speaking turns that normal conversational exchange requires. After all, you can't process information and send it at the same time. So far, so good—the mother appears to be shaping the infant's responses in the direction required later when he becomes truly verbal. But there is another hitch or variant in the mother-infant vocal conversational system. When we tried to replicate the findings of Catherine Bateson showing that by three months mothers and infants had already evolved a pattern of alternating vocalizing turns, we did confirm her finding that this does indeed occur sometimes.[6] However, we found that the more common vocalizing pattern during play was that mother and infant were taking turns but were vocalizing in unison.[7] They seemed to be "moved" to make sound together. Furthermore, this vocalizing in unison, or "chorusing," as Rudolph Schaffer calls it for a later age,[8] was more likely to occur as the interaction became more lively and engaging. It seems to serve more as a bonding function than as an exchange of information.

So once again with vocalization, we find the mother and infant using different patterns of interactions from those used later in development. On the mother's part, as with facial expressions, we also find similar alterations and exaggerations in time and degree of the vocal stimulus world provided for the infant.

Gaze. Here too, the adult cultural "rules" regulating how people gaze at each other in a social interaction go out the window when we consider how mothers gaze at their infants. The first rule in our culture is that two people do not remain gazing into each other's eyes (mutual gaze) for long. Mutual gaze is a potent interpersonal event which greatly increases general arousal and evokes strong feelings and potential actions of some kind, depending on the interactants and the situation. It rarely lasts more than several seconds. In fact, two people do not gaze into each other's eyes without speech for over ten or so seconds unless they are going to fight or make love or already are. Not so with mother and infant. They can remain locked in mutual gaze for thirty seconds or more.

The second rule to go out the window concerns how adults coordinate their gazing and speaking. Generally (there are ethnic exceptions), in a conversation the listener looks at the speaker most of the time. The speaker in the meanwhile generally looks at the listener for a moment or two when he starts speaking. He then looks away as he continues talking and only checks back to the listener's face with occasional glances (to get some feedback). Toward the end of his speaking turn, he again looks at the listener to signal that he is about to finish and relinquish the floor. The ex-speaker, now listener, will then remain looking at the new speaker's face.[9]

During play interactions, mothers invariably gaze and vocalize at the infant simultaneously. Furthermore, they spend upwards of 70 percent of play time gazing at their infant with an average gaze duration of about 20 seconds, which is extremely long. During feeding the mothers also look at their infants about 70 percent of the time but with shorter gazes more in the range of about 12 seconds a gaze.[10] However, during feeding the mother will not gaze and vocalize at the infant simultaneously. As we shall see, this combination is too strong an "invitation" to play and is likely to interrupt the feeding. Accordingly, while feeding, if the mother is looking at her infant she will actively inhibit vocalizing.

In comparison to the adult signal system, then, during play the mother gazes as if she were the listener when in fact she is usually the speaker. During feeding she gazes more like a speaker, but is quiet. It is worth wondering how in the world the infant will acquire the appropriate mature forms of the human communicative system when he begins life exposed to such variants of that system.

Face presentations and other head movements. There is nothing quite like the sudden appearance of a face to capture attention or hold it. Peek-a-boo, one of the all-time favorite international infant games, is of course a repetition of disappearances and reappearances of the face. This game is the reliable stand-by to hold attention and produce delight. Peek-a-boo games where the mother uses a screen (a blanket or her hands, say) to hide and then show her face begin in earnest some time around the fourth month or later. The infant, of course, remains a spectator and the mother the sole player until considerably later. An earlier form of peek-a-boo can be played without the use of any screens. It consists simply of a series of presentations of the full face toward the infant's, interspersed with turning the face to the side, or down, or pulling the head way back, and then representing the full face again, at roughly the same distance as the last presentation. When trying to hold attention or engender delight, much of a mother's head movement conforms to this simple plan. A common example suffices: the mother lowers her head as if looking at the floor, revealing to the infant the top of her head and says something like "eeeeee-yáh" and sharply brings her head back up to the full-face position on the accented "yáh." She then lowers her head again for the next round. In this situation the head does not disappear and reappear as in more formal peek-a-boo, but the full-face presentation does. The consistency and frequency of this kind of sequence are impressive and are built into a large array of the social activities a mother engages the baby in. For instance, there is the repetitious way a mother often asks a question: "Are you hungry?" "Are you?

Huh?" "Yeah, I think you are." Each time she verbalizes one of those questions she may bring her head and body forward and tilt her head up to show her full face as she speaks. Then, in between questions, she moves back and lets her head settle downward. Each question may be accompanied by a distinct and simultaneous face presentation.

Repeated face presentations even get built into apparently unrelated play activities. For instance, in the "vibrate the lips against the infant's belly" game, characteristically after each lunge forward to tickle the belly, the mother leans back and straightens up with a face presentation, usually a mock-surprise expression, which punctuates each tickle, before she dives for the belly again. In fact, from watching the infant, it is often hard to tell which event is more wonderous, the belly tickle or the animated face presentation that follows.

Perhaps the most crucial feature of this format of maternal attention-holding behavior is that each serial face presentation is accompanied by some facial display, an expression. Accordingly, the almost continuous series of exaggeratedly discrete and punctuated face presentations becomes a vehicle for the sequential presentation of a varying array of facial expressions. These face presentations differ from those seen in adult-adult interactions in that they have more discrete boundaries, more particularly marked behavioral rests or "silences" surrounding them, and are more slowly and exaggeratedly performed so that each separate presentation with its display is thrown into higher relief for the infant.

As far as other head movements are concerned, the common feature of all the other infant-elicited social behaviors applies—exaggeration or fullness of display. It applies to a variety of head movements that will ultimately assume signal importance: head nodding up and down, head wagging side to side, head cocking from one side to the other, and head averting of often theatrical proportions.

Proxemics. Among adults and children there exists an entity called interpersonal space. To oversimplify, each of us walks about surrounded by a psychological "bubble," a certain distance from our bodies; if the bubble is burst by someone coming too close, "penetrating" it, this causes us to experience discomfort and usually to step away. The intimate distance in our culture is roughly a couple of feet, face-to-face. There are of course large individual differences and even larger cultural differences. Nonetheless, the phenomenon exists in all cultures. Only in the course of an intimate interaction is the violation of the distance expected, accepted, and even pleasurable.

Most adults, even complete strangers, act as if there were no intimate distance barrier for babies, or for themselves with babies. They think nothing of rushing in at first meeting to make nose-to-nose contact. Many adults, such as aunts, who are disliked by infants for unknown reasons are often notorious for this kind of space-violating behavior, much to the upset of the infant and his mother. What is more, they usually remain oblivious to the effect they have just had.

Infants do not like to be encroached upon in this manner. There is an important literature on the infant's aversive response to objects which loom toward his face and much evidence suggests that this reaction is innate, deriving from reflexes evolved for the survival need of protecting the face and eyes.[11] In any event, mothers show a somewhat casual regard for this infant reaction. Many of the mother's face presentations, head movements, touches, and games play havoc with the infant's looming responses (which might well be considered a forerunner of his development of an intimate space barrier). She may rapidly zoom in on him to kiss or pretend-bite his nose, then pull way back, far out of intimate range, and then come in again, looming closer but at the same time performing facial displays and emitting sounds that rivet his visual attention so that the looming response is inhibited, or at any rate not performed. This constant disregard by mothers of adult spatial conventions may be important in preparing the infant to tolerate, or even more, to engage socially within an intimate distance. Later affiliative behaviors such as kissing and snuggling may partially depend on the successful outcome of these first experiences.

INTEGRATION OF SEPARATE BEHAVIORS

The separate behaviors described above are generally elicited together in one coordinated package. The mother performs a facial display, while vocalizing, while gazing and within the framework of a discrete head movement-face presentation. To an observer, and perhaps the infant, the multi-modal event is experienced as a single communicative or expressive unit. Nonetheless, each element in her performance can be performed in isolation, though it rarely is. However, to understand better how and to what extent each behavioral element influences the infant, it would be experimentally "clean" to isolate each element or to even present separate elements recombined in various ways.

My first crude attempts at such experiments were total flops—but instructive for that very reason. When we asked a mother to perform typical facial displays when the infant was not looking at her, or to direct them slightly (45 degrees) away from the baby, the mother felt embarrassed or ridiculous and most often the result was general laughter at the funny faces. When we asked a mother to talk to the infant as if she were looking at him, but without actually looking at him, it resulted in a difficult and stilted acting performance. Last, when we asked mothers to gaze but not speak or move their bodies or faces, it always resulted in upset mothers, infants, or researchers.

We abandoned this form of experiment. However, others in a laboratory setting have devised a variety of such experimental manipulation of the separate stimuli a mother provides. Two will be mentioned since they build to a larger point. Tronick and his colleagues asked mothers to alternate between normal active "alive" facial and vocal behavior and going deadpan and silent while gazing at the baby. The infants' main reaction was one of distress and aversion to the deadpan face.[12] (Before the infant turned off, he did many fascinating things to get the mother to "behave.") Here we can see the unnaturalness for the baby as well as for the mother of inhibiting one or several particular elements of the integrated display of simultaneous social behaviors.

The other fascinating experiment is directed to the issue of whether the infant expects different stimuli emanating from the mother to be integrated in a predictable fashion—whether and which things reliably belong together in the human world. The question was, when is a mother's voice supposed to come from the same place or direction as the mother's mouth or face? Through the clever arrangement of placing a mother behind soundproof glass in full view of her infant, and having her speak into a microphone connected to two loudspeakers on either side of the infant, the researchers could make her voice appear to come from any direction up to 90 degrees away from her face on either side, by unbalancing the loudness of the two speakers. By the time infants were three months of age, but not before, they became very upset when the mother's voice came from any direction more removed than 15 degrees from her face position.[13]

Faces and their voices should go together or, rather, come from the same place. No doubt there are many other such things that should "go together" which we, as adults, take for granted as part of the world of human behavior—say, certain expressions and certain kinds of vocalizations. In fact, for adults, many of the nuances of expression result from the leaving out of one or more expected elements in a constellation of behaviors that make up an anticipated and known display. The infant, however, must first acquire experience and knowledge of a basic repertoire of expressive displays. The caregiver's characteristic way of performing and integrating the separate behaviors speeds the infant along in this process.

During these first six months of life the infant begins to lay the foundation of one of his most highly developed areas of expertise, namely, "reading" the signals and expressions of other people's behaviors. By the end of this short period of life he will be able to discriminate most of the basic human expressive displays. In addition, he will already know the basic conventions and signals that regulate the flow of a vocal interaction.

WHY DO BABIES ELICIT THESE BEHAVIORS?

This question raises all the problematical issues of innateness versus learning. Whenever we see a set of behaviors that is probably used by all societies in a particular natural human situation, and which has had thousands of generations of evolutionary history to fashion an adaptive purpose, we wonder to what extent its acquisition is built upon some biologically innate base. We can only sneak up on a tentative answer. Certainly the sight of a baby is not an innate releaser in the strictest sense that students of animal behavior use the term—that, on sight, a fixed behavioral pattern will almost invariably be evoked from the adult. Yet sometimes it almost looks that way. Other authors

(Decarie) have noted how some people (usually women and girls) seem almost irresistibly drawn to baby carriages in the park or on the sidewalk. And, once there, to the amusement or annoyance of the mother, they stick their faces into the carriage and launch into a full-blown performance of infant-elicited social behaviors. Still the fact remains that some adults and some parents do it far less than others. Some do it only with their own child but rarely with another's. Some parents have a fuller or smaller repertoire of these behaviors, and some show greater or lesser degrees of fullness of display than others. Some can do it more fully in one modality than another, say more in vocalizations but less so in making faces. Yet, in spite of this variability, which is in large part a function of who the infant is, some form of these behaviors is present in almost all mothers. It is a highly unusual caregiver who always behaves toward an infant as she would toward an adult, and a very ineffective, in fact, aversive one, as we shall discover.

We often talk loosely about someone who is a "natural" with babies. It is an impression that is quickly gathered and usually rests on the evaluation of at least three things: the extent of their repertoire of infant-elicited social behaviors; the manner of performance of these behaviors (richness, variety, and fullness of displays); and the subtlety of timing of these behaviors so that they are most effective.

Our term, "infant-elicited," is complex. I certainly do not mean that the caregiver behaviors are obligatorily evoked or that wide variability in response is not the rule. I mean simply that a strong tendency exists in the vast majority of us to respond in a fairly stereotypic and predictable way.

"Babyness." Over three decades ago, Konrad Lorenz suggested that if the very young of any species required special parenting experience to provide them with the socialization necessary for survival, they better have some means of making sure that this kind of parenting behavior was forthcoming. The survival of the species depended on it. He suggested that one of the possible means was for the very young to look quite different from the mature members of the species. The physical characteristics that distinguished the young from the mature would serve as innate releasers for caregiving behaviors from

parents. He went further to point out that the physical differences between young and mature are remarkably similar in most species requiring specialized caregiving behaviors to promote socialization and thus survival (dogs, cats, birds, man).

The constellation of distinguishing features of the young, which together he called "babyness," are: a large head in proportion to body size; a large and protruding forehead in relation to the rest of the face; large eyes relative to face size; the eyes positioned below the horizontal midline of the face; and round protruding cheeks.

Both Lorenz and Eibl-Eibesfeldt have commented that these criteria of babyness are essentially the same for all the species mentioned and that this may explain the appeal of cuteness or cuddliness that most young animals have for humans. It may also explain why baby animals can elicit behaviors similar to those we reserve for human infants. Eibl-Eibesfeldt further points out how the commercial world exploits the appeal of babyness features by exaggerating in cartoons or postcards the large eyes or round cheeks to enhance the appeal. This observation is of some clinical importance because in this fashion the society has some leeway in molding idealized standards of what an appealing infant ought to look like—much as our cultural standards of adult beauty are molded.

What an infant looks like, however, is certainly not the whole story of the eliciting power of infants. There is also what the infant does with his configuration of physical features, his expressive movements: the special smiles, the varieties of eye brightening, the open mouth with the head thrown back and the tongue thrust out. This last behavior in one series of observations proved to be far more potent than the smile in evoking a flurry of positively toned social behaviors from mothers. To experience the evocative power of this behavior, have someone open their mouth wide and stick out their tongue while looking at you and throw their head up but bring it toward you (or do it in the mirror to yourself). Depending on who it comes from, it evokes different emotions from sexy to disgusting, but in any event it is potent. When performed by an infant, though, it generally elicits quite positive sensations from mothers.

In any case, infant behaviors (anatomy in motion) are just as likely as static anatomical configurations are to have some biological loading as elicitors of this subset of behaviors we are talking about. Much more study is needed here to know how much of the eliciting power of infants is biologically predetermined and how much is the way they look as against what they do.

Who performs these behaviors? The list of performers is large: mothers and fathers, of course; parents with their first, next, and last child; grandparents and great-grandparents; childless adults and adolescents, both boys and girls; and prepubescent children, both boys and girls with or without younger siblings. We see that learning from prior experience with infants is relatively unimportant. The behaviors are not the sole province of one sex. There is no specified developmental period of the life span, such as from puberty to menopause, when these behaviors are biologically or hormonally triggered—and outside of which they cannot occur. Unlike some animal species where one type of member of the species is biologically primed for a given period for this purpose, in man this specialized ability is extended to include almost all its members both male and female from middle childhood through old age. The implications of this arrangement are that we have enormous flexibility (excluding other constraints) in institutionalizing any number of social groupings to substitute for or, simply and more commonly, to add to the biological mother's role in providing appropriate social stimulation for infants during their first six months of life. (Even before the advent of the bottle there was no overriding reason why the provider of milk had to be the same person as the provider of social stimuli, and she has not been in all societies.) The minimal need for learning or practicing these behaviors permits us much of the impressive flexibility of having such a wide variety of societal members to draw on, at any time for any circumstance, as adequate sources of human social stimulation for infants.

Having said that much, I shall complicate the picture by taking back with one hand part of what was just given with the other. Involved here are two partially unanswered questions: When in childhood do children first show the ability to perform these behaviors? Is this subset of behaviors more readily elicitable from girls and women and, if so, why?

Starting with the first question, Fullard and Relling tried to find out at what age people began to *prefer* looking at an infant's face as compared to an adult's face.[14] They did this by showing two slides, one of an adult and one of an infant, to males and females who ranged in age from seven years through adulthood. The two slides (shown simultaneously) included adult and infant animals' faces as well as adult and infant human faces. The subjects were simply asked which of the faces they preferred. It turned out that girls began to prefer infant faces (both human and animal) beginning between ages twelve and fourteen, and kept that preference through adulthood. Boys began to show the same change in preference about two years later but to a weaker extent, as did men compared to women.

Since the ages twelve to fourteen correspond roughly to the establishment of puberty in girls, with boys maturing a year or so later, these studies suggest a biological or more specifically hormonal role for the preference change. The authors are careful to point out, however, that a variety of social factors potentially influencing such a preference come strongly into play at these ages.

So far there are no definitive studies "asking" when children are capable of performing some recognizable version of this subset of behaviors. But a good deal of anecdotal evidence suggests it occurs quite early, in middle childhood. A preliminary study we have piloted suggests that both boys and girls as early as six years of age (long before any biological issues of puberty are at stake) show these behaviors toward live human infants and even more toward live baby animals. The repertoire in these children appears to be relatively limited but includes at least raising the pitch of the voice; repetitious vocalizations; baby talk; prolonged gaze; making some faces including eyebrow raising and lip protrusions; and a variety of touching behaviors including nuzzling, patting, stroking, and kissing—many of which involve violating intimate distance boundaries with impunity. It is interesting that these childhood behaviors are not necessarily present or so marked in doll play, where most often the majority of time is spent in task-oriented parental behaviors —feeding, changing, bathing, teaching-scolding—rather than in purely social, though imaginary, interactions with an inanimate partner.

It seems likely, then, that infant-elicited social behaviors are already part of a child's behavioral capability long before puberty. Whether and when they choose to use them is another question. This is in keeping with observations of an infant's daily life among the !Kung bushmen of the Kalahari Desert. In that society mothers carry their infants around in a sling so that the infant and mother have little face-to-face contact or play during most of the working day. Mel Konner, who studied these people, mentioned that one of the sources of social stimulation for the infant in this position came from prepubescent children, usually girls, who frequently ran up to the infant to have a quick and lively, but unsustained, bout of exchanges, which included the performance of our behavioral subset.[15] It further turns out that the infant in his hip sling is positioned at almost exactly the eye level of these prepubescent children—the ideal situation to promote the social interaction.

Our second unanswered question regards females versus males. It is quite obvious that in our culture, biological differences notwithstanding, females appear to have a greater readiness to respond to babyness in the laboratory and to infants in daily life. They also generally have a more extensive and richer repertoire of infant-elicited social behaviors and are less inhibited in manifesting this subset. We do not know if different learning, modeling, and social conditions would equalize or reverse this situation. No documented society has yet tried.

In summary, the picture looks like this: The variations in peer-directed social behaviors that I call infant-elicited social behaviors are already present in middle childhood and capable of being performed by boys and girls by the age of six or so. It is not until the biological and social changes of puberty set in, however, that there is a preference or perhaps "push" to choose and often seek out infants to elicit these special behaviors. Thus, at the point when parenthood becomes biologically possible, the appropriate behavioral repertoire that has been present but partially dormant receives the needed impetus. The cultural factors that strengthen the females' utilization and performance of these behaviors is so varied and pervasive in this society that it has been impossible to isolate any definite biological factors leading to differential behavior.

In any event, men, children, and all adults past childrearing age are available as secondary caregivers and potentially primary ones if a group or society so chooses under pressure of survival or for other reasons.

A clinical issue. As brand-new parents we are biologically (and culturally) predisposed to respond to the normal newborn, his facial configuration and behaviors. But suppose what we see isn't what we expected. Suppose the baby is born with some deformity of the head, face, eyes, or mouth that disrupts "the" configuration. The parents often experience an interruption or partial inhibition in fully "going out" to their infant. A similar thing may happen in a far more common and milder way. Suppose the newborn is simply ugly compared to an expected standard. What constitutes "ugliness" in a baby is anything that is discrepant with the idealized babyness: a low brow (the large protruding forehead is not present), small eyes, and so on. These realities are hardly trivial to the parents, and may hurt. Good looks and ugliness are partially taboo subjects, but they are capable of causing parental pain. Most often the issue is never mentioned or is joked away and only causes a temporary impediment to fully loving the child right off the bat. The sensitive nurse or doctor is aware of these feelings and often deals with them easily, to the relief of the parents.

Another look at our evolutionary history may again prove helpful, or at least provocative. Most animal mothers, including those who are superb mothers by their own yardsticks, are biologically primed to provide their newborns with maternal caregiving. Nonetheless, they will inhibit their maternal behaviors (or instinct if you prefer) and leave to die any offspring who do not seem sufficiently normal. Similar behavior has also been reported in several so-called primitive societies. The advantage to the survival of the species is clear, despite the abhorrence that such events evoke in us.

We have taken this unpleasant side trip only to wonder if the mothers we see who are faced with an infant deformed in some, even minor, way are not the unwilling victims of an involuntary inhibition of their caregiving. An inhibition, even if small and temporary, to which they are the unwitting legatee of evolution. Whatever the reasons, these realities and feelings are real and worthy of greater attention.

So far in this chapter we have looked at infant-elicited social behaviors and followed several sidepaths through issues of their nature, possible origin, and development in different people. We return now to the central reason for focusing on them to begin with. These behaviors are the mother's most crucial tools to regulate her half of the interaction with the infant. By regulate, I mean to start up, to maintain and modulate, and to terminate an interaction, as well as constantly to readjust the infant's level of attention, arousal, and emotional tone. The way she sequences and times her behaviors to create different tempos, themes, and variations on themes will enhance the infant's understanding of human communication and emotional expressiveness.

Before studying these issues, however, we must first turn to the infant and examine his repertoire of behaviors. After all, we are talking about a two-person interaction, which is only comprehensible as a dyadic relationship.

3 / The Infant's Repertoire

The infant comes into the world bringing formidable capabilities to establish human relatedness. Immediately he is a partner in shaping his first and foremost relationships. His social equipment, though extraordinary, is obviously immature. However, the notion of immaturity carries some excess baggage that gets in our way. The label "immature" cannot be a green light to dismiss a behavior until its more mature version arrives; nor can it be an invitation to focus on the developmental process itself— that mysterious series of transformations into maturity. Ultimately any human being is simply what he is at the moment we find him. The behaviors of a three-month-old are totally mature and fully accomplished three-month-old behaviors. The same is true at two years, ten years, twenty-one years. You can draw the line where you wish, depending on what human capabilities are of particular interest or under scrutiny.

In taking this relativistic position I do not mean to minimize the forceful reality of development and growth. But where the interaction between two people, and how it works and fits, is of primary interest, the degree of maturity of either partner's contribution to the interaction becomes a secondary issue. Even more important, though a mother well understands, intellectually, that her infant is immature, and often prays he will grow up faster, she cannot enter into a full spontaneous relationship with him unless all that is put aside emotionally. Like any other important person in her life, he is what he is, interacting with what he has, at the moment he is encountered.

What then are the infant's social "tools," the perceptual and motor abilities that lead and permit him to engage in social inter-

33

changes? My list will not be comprehensive and will not cata-
logue all that an infant can do and perceive. Instead it will emphasize only those events that bear on the establishment of
human relatedness, communication, and emotional exchanges
during social interactions in the first six months of life, when the
infant is so sharply focused on the human stimulus world that
his primary caregiver provides.

GAZE

What is interesting for an infant to look at? It was only a
little over a decade ago that the importance of gaze as a cardinal
social and bonding behavior began to be appreciated. At birth,
the visual motor system (looking at and seeing) comes immediately into operation. The newborn cannot only see but arrives
with reflexes that allow him to follow and fixate upon an object.
Without any previous experience he can follow a moving object
with his eyes and head and can hold his gaze on it. This is easily
demonstrated in most alert newborns. Many of them, within
minutes of birth, will alertly follow with their eyes and head an
object passed across their visual field. No learning is necessary.
But what do they see? There is an all-important difference between looking and seeing, as there is between listening and hearing.

Is the newborn immediately inundated with a chaotic and
overwhelming world? A world where there is light and dark and
angles and lines and patterns but no meaningful objects, no way
to know where one thing leaves off and another begins, no way
to distinguish the human from the inanimate. Such a "world"
can exist. In the 1920s the surgeon, M. von Senden, came up
with some fascinating findings. Von Senden had the rare opportunity to remove cataracts surgically from the eyes of adults who
had been blind since birth because of them but who otherwise
had perfectly good visual systems. The results were astounding.
The patients were given sight for the first time but could not see.
Most of them "saw" quite well but found the visual world con-
fusing, nonsensical, and a painful sensory experience. Many
wished to be blind again. Only slowly did the objects in the
visual world begin to conform to, and at the same time alter,
their previous conceptions, schemas that had been built up with

their other senses over the years of blindness. A comfortable "fit" came gradually.[1]

Why is it not this way for the newborn? First, and most obviously, the baby does not arrive into life with preformed notions of the world's objects. It is all new. There are no preconceptions or established systems of things to clash against his visual sensations. Thus, there can be no confusion in the sense of disorienting discrepancies or painful reappraisals. He is endowed with the tendency to seek out stimulation—and he is organized so that he will tend to order his experiences into progressively larger, more complex, and more encompassing hierarchies. Such is his nature. So long as the stimuli do not overwhelm him, he goes about his momentous task with intensity and pleasure. So rather than having to reorganize his object world as did Von Senden's patients, he has the more extraordinary, yet less encumbered, task of having to create anew the entire object world. Each infant has to create pictures within his own mind of the world of objects and people.

This may sound like the now discarded view of the infant arriving into the world as a blank page to be written on by his experiences with life. This is neither my view nor the case. The infant arrives with an array of innately determined perceptual predilections, motor patterns, cognitive or thinking tendencies, and abilities for emotional expressiveness and perhaps recognition. Nonetheless, for the line of inquiry we are now pursuing, none of these innate "orderings" of the world are of enough specificity or fixity to make the newborn encounter the dissonance or confusion described in the newly sighted patients.

The infant can readily be overwhelmed by excessive stimulation. However, he is "designed" so that he occupies a niche in nature with his mother which tends to strike a balance between protecting him from excessive stimuli and at the same time assuring his exposure to enough stimulation from the visual world. One of the first "design features" assuring this balance is that the infant can only focus well on objects about eight inches away. He cannot clearly see objects much farther away or much closer. They get out of focus and presumably become fuzzy. So, right away, the newborn's sharp visual world is restricted to a perimeter of roughly eight or so inches. A strong light from a good distance does make an infant turn away, but he will generally be unaffected by most other visual events outside of this focus range.

For the first several weeks after birth, the majority of the baby's awake alert time is spent in and around feeding and somewhat less in diapering or bathing. What will he see? It turns out that when the infant is in the normal breast- or bottle-feeding position his eyes are almost exactly eight inches from his mother's eyes (if she is facing him).[2] We have found that, during feeding, mothers spend about 70 percent of the time facing and looking at their infants. Accordingly, what he is most likely to look at and see is his mother's face, especially her eyes. (Several earlier theories assumed that the first and most important object the infant sees is the breast. This is certainly not correct since during suckling the breast is too close to be in focus.) Thus the arrangement of anatomy, normal positioning, and visual competence dictated by natural design all point to the mother's face as an initial focal point of importance for the infant's early construction of his salient visual world, and a starting point for the formation of his early human relatedness.

A second line of evidence also indicates the importance of gaze in early human relatedness. Ahrens and Spitz noted that infants of about three months showed more interest and smiled more at faces presented to them full face front, compared to profiles, or to other objects.[3] The essence of these observations was distilled into the following experiment. Infants were presented with drawings of a variety of forms, including faces and other objects. They seemed to prefer a simple two-dimensional line for the drawing of a face. Furthermore, the crucial facial features that accounted for the preference were two eyelike, large dots correctly placed within a larger oval. These findings suggested to many workers that the infant was born with an innate preference for the human face—or at least some of its features.

An innate predilection for a specific visual configuration is no small matter. It implies that some scheme or "picture" of a human face is encoded in our genes, reflected in our nervous systems, and ultimately expresses itself in our behavior without any previous specific learning experiences. A productive controversy was launched, and the issue at stake boiled down to this question: Was it the specific configuration of the face, the face gestalt, that was so interesting to infants, or was it any visual stimulus of the same size containing the same amount of angularity, light and shade contrast, complexity of pattern, curvilinearity, and so on. Through the ingenious early work of Fantz and others, it had become possible to find out fairly exactly what infants were drawn to gaze at.[4]

For a while some experiments leaned to one side of this nature versus nurture controversy, and others tilted the opposite way. The studies of Friedman and Haaf and Bell resolved the issue by carefully controlling the various separate elements of the stimulus, such as complexity and shade contrast.[5] They found that what the infant preferred was not the face configuration itself, but rather any visual stimulus that contained certain qualities and quantities of the stimulus elements mentioned, whether or not this combination of elements came in the configuration of a face or something else. From one point of view, the distinction is quite important because of its implications. Practically, however, the distinction is moot: of all the visual objects in the universe that the average infant is likely to encounter in the "average expectable environment," the human face comes about as close as anything will come to providing just the right combination of captivating stimulus elements. Furthermore, its special interest is founded on a biological basis by virtue of the infant's innate bias for certain kinds and amounts of stimulation. The situation is something like innateness "once removed." Other studies have shown that the sharp angles provided by the corners of the eyes as well as the light-dark contrast of pupil and eye white (sclera) and of eyebrow and skin are especially fascinating to the infant. From the very beginning, then, the infant is "designed" to find the human face fascinating, and the mother is led to attract as much interest as possible to her already "interesting" face.

A change in gaze. At some point around the sixth week, the infant's visual motor system achieves a developmental landmark that often catapults the social interaction with mother onto a new level. What happens is subtle. The infant simply becomes capable of visually fixating his mother's eyes and holding the fixation with eye widening and eye brightening.[6] As for the mother, she experiences for the first time the very certain impression that the infant is really looking at *her*, even more, *into* her eyes. The effect of this can be dramatic. The mother may experience that she and the baby are finally "connected." Perhaps for the first time, or at least more completely than before, the mother feels that the baby is a fully responsive human being and they are engaged in a real relationship. Most often mothers cannot identify the change. At best, the more observant say that the infant looks at her differently. In any event, beginning about this time the mother's behavior becomes markedly more social—vocally, facially, and in all the other ways mentioned before. Truly social play interactions involving both partners now begin in earnest.

Consequences of the early maturation of gaze. By the end of the third month, another developmental milestone is reached. The visual motor system has become essentially mature. First of all, his visual world is no longer limited to an eight-inch "bubble." The infant's focal distance has a range almost as extensive as adults. The infant can track the mother as she leaves, approaches, and moves about the room. His communicative network is thus vastly extended.

There are other striking aspects of this precocity. To appreciate them fully, it is necessary to review briefly what is involved in gazing, or the workings of the visual motor system. Gazing involves two quite different things: sight, one of the senses; and a motor act, movement of the eyes and usually the head also, to pursue or hold the visual target. These two functions working together provide visual perception with a unique feature. You can turn sight off or on at will. By closing the eyes, or simply turning the eyes away or down, the target object disappears. It can also be made to "reappear." In comparison, the ears have no earlids, and tuning out sound is not so simple as turning on or off sight. So clearly, gaze has an unusual feature as a mode for dealing with the external world.

By the end of the third month, the infant is about as good as an adult in rapidly moving his eyes to pursue an object or hold a fixation, and he is equally capable of quickly accommodating his eyes to bring objects into focus. This developmental landmark is extraordinary when contrasted with the immaturity of most of his other systems of communication and the regulation of interpersonal contact, for instance, speech, gesture, locomotion, manipulation of objects. (The infant's control over two other motor systems is quite mature by this point: sucking and head movements. We shall consider head movements below, but sucking itself never achieves a full or enduring status as a communicative system.)

The vagaries of man's developmental timetable, which ordains the early maturation of the visual motor system, result in a striking situation. The dyadic gazing interaction between mother and infant involves the interplay between two humans with essentially equal control and use of the same modality. It should be recalled that one member of the pair is only 3 to 4 months old. It is little wonder that early gazing behaviors have attracted more and more attention.

By the end of the third month the infant's mature motor control of gaze direction gives him essentially complete control over what he will see. His perceptual input becomes largely of his own choosing. He can veto or censor or titrate the amount and kind of visual stimulation he takes in from what is available in the outside world. When the outside stimulation is another human being, the infant is in the position to help regulate the degree or level of relatedness and to influence the flow of interpersonal behaviors. He becomes a true partner.

The shift to objects. Toward the end of the first half year of life, the infant's love affair with the human face and voice and touch is partially replaced by a consuming interest in objects to reach for, grasp, and manipulate. This turn in interest is made possible by the last developmental landmark that will concern us here: the infant's hand-eye coordination, which has now come of age.

Once this happens, the mother-infant interaction becomes quite different. Their play interactions become more a triadic affair among mother, infant, and object. Different behaviors with different goals come into being. The human caregiver is now in the wings rather than at center stage of the infant's attention during the object-play sessions that now dominate his alert waking day. Presumably, the developmental "work" accomplished during the earlier phase—learning the basics of the nature of human things—is largely over, and the next phase of learning the nature of object things is ushered in. The caregiver remains essential of course during this phase too, but not in the same capacity.

Head behaviors. How a head is held or postured or how it is moved can be potent social signals among adults. The same is no less true for infants. I mentioned before that motor control of the head matures roughly in step with the precocious maturation of the visual motor system. It is almost impossible to consider gaze behaviors without considering at the same time head movements (as distinct from eye movements). The head and eyes generally move together, but not always and not always to the same degree. Head movements and gaze shifts are generally coordinated, although each adds a separate and different communicative impact to the jointly performed behaviors. In considering these coordinated behaviors it is necessary to hold in mind two different experiences: the infant as performer and the caregiver as recipient.

Starting from the infant's side, there are three main head positions—gaze directions relative to the mother's face.[7] In the central position the infant is gazing at the mother's face and his face is directly facing hers or only slightly turned away to either side. The infant views the mother with foveal vision. The fovea is that functionally central part of the retina where form and pattern perception are possible, and the infant thus sees the exact configuration of facial features presented by the mother. The next position is the peripheral. The infant is not looking directly at the mother but can "see" her out of the "corner" of his eye. His head is turned anywhere from 15 degrees to almost 90 degrees away from mother. He no longer has foveal vision and cannot make out the configuration of her facial features, but he does have peripheral vision of her face. Form perception is lost, but perception of motion, speed, and direction is retained. So in this very common position the infant can monitor the mother's head movements and changes in her facial expression. These also involve motion—even though the qualitative nature of the facial change may be lost. Accordingly, he has not lost contact and can perceive and react to her.[8] The third position is total loss of visual contact. This is generally achieved by the baby's turning his head past 90 degrees away or lowering it, or some combination of both. In this position, form perception and motion perception are both lost.

These three main positions can be broken down into finer gradations, but the central point is that in each different position the infant has a different sensory (visual) and motor (head position) experience relative to the caregiver. So each position provides the infant with a different sensori-motor "experience" of being with his mother which is under his control.

From the mother's side, the nature and degree of the infant's gaze direction and head turning are of great importance as a signal. First there is the vital issue of whether or not the baby is looking into the mother's eyes. If the baby is and also is directly facing her, that is one thing. If, however, he is looking at her but has turned his head slightly away, say 10-15 degrees, that is another matter. Gazing "sideways" has the character of an equivocal or ambivalent signal. It contains the contradictory components of contact with the eyes and aversion or flight with the head. With infants under six months (compared to adults), it is an unstable position that rapidly gets resolved one way or the other, into full facing with eye contact or further head aversion with loss of eye contact.

Turning the head away to the side is almost invariably interpreted as a signal of aversion or flight. (We shall later encounter a notable exception or variant where it is a gleeful invitation to the mother to chase.) In any event, face aversion can be considered part of an innate avoidance pattern which the newborn shows when an object looms toward his face. The face aversion we are dealing with here is a later avatar of that reflex pressed into a social function. The signal function such a pattern serves depends on its fullness of display which, in this case, is easily measured in degree and speed of aversion. The further and faster the infant averts his face the more the mother will assume he does not like something. This applies to a visual stimulus such as her face, as well as to a spoonful of some hated food.

The gaze and face aversions involved in peripheral monitoring are not complete avoidance or flight actions. They are akin to "intention movements" that reflect and signal the internal motivational state of the infant, and still allow him to view and react to the mother's movements, thus maintaining interactive commerce with her. The completed flight pattern would involve a full turning away with loss of all visual contact. This generally marks the termination of the interactive episode or play period.

Head lowering is another effective avoidance behavior. It

appears to achieve a more definitive, if temporary, cut-off of the interaction than does face aversion to the side. This action immediately breaks all visual contact while side aversions maintain the peripheral monitoring. Head lowering is a promising area for more research. How early, for instance, does head lowering evolve into later forms of surrender, giving up, signing off, and such? We certainly often enough see infants lower their heads and go limp after they have given up fighting off overstimulation.

We have already seen that some infant head movements appear to belong to approach patterns. Bringing the head forward especially while tilting the face up is enormously appealing to mothers and is invariably interpreted as an affectively positive act of approach.

As early as the third to fourth month of life, then, the infant is capable of the clear performance of mixed or ambivalent head behaviors: he takes, so to speak, an element from one motivational pattern, and another element from a second and conflicting pattern, to produce a conglomerate behavior with a third and separate meaning of its own. For instance, when an infant breaks gaze and averts his face partially (say 45 degrees) but raises his head and tilts his face up, it is generally treated by the mother as a holding action. The mother keeps performing and trying to get the infant's full attention, reading his behavior almost as an invitation for greater efforts on her part. If, on the other hand, an infant breaks gaze and averts his face in exactly the same way, but lowers instead of raises his head and face, it is generally interpreted as a temporary cut-off. The mother will stop performing and resume only after changing her approach strategy.

FACIAL EXPRESSIONS

Charles Darwin was one of the first observers of animals to recognize that the survival of highly social species could depend as much on their ability to communicate with one another as on their anatomical equipment for fighting or flight. Since he was also the first to see clearly man's evolutionary relationship to other social animals, he concluded that man, too, had to be equipped with the ability to send and receive important social cues bearing on survival. It was then only a short leap to ask how man acquired these species-specific expressive signals. Were these behaviors inborn and part of the evolutionary process as were anatomical features, or were they all learned? This question led Darwin to the far-reaching insight that the observation of the human newborn's expressive behavior provided a window into what was innate in man. Charlesworth and Kreutzer have beautifully summarized Darwin's findings as well as the hundred years of research in this area which have followed his groundbreaking but until recently neglected book.[9] They conclude that Darwin's essential findings hold up remarkably well. Specifically, Darwin concluded that the facial expressions of the basic emotions of pleasure, displeasure, anger, fear, joy, sorrow, and disgust were either present at birth or, when they appeared a few months later, reflected the unfolding of innate tendencies that were little influenced by socialization. He was less certain about the role of socialization for the more complex emotions.

More recent observers have been impressed with the large number of facial expressions newborns can make which appear to be identical to expressions seen on the faces of adults, expressions such as intense visual interest; cunning and wisdom; wry humor; complicated contortions of disgust or rejection; quizzical frowns and serene smiles. It should be stressed, however, that no one suggests that with such expressions the newborn experiences anything at all, let alone internal feelings comparable to those generally associated with the expressions in adults.

Although these early expressions, which are certainly reflexive, require much more rigorous study and categorization, nonetheless their mere presence is provocative. First, regarding "innateness," the presence of these expressions lends strong evidence to the notion that the infant is born with a surprising degree of facial neuromuscular maturity and, furthermore, that the movement of facial muscles is partly integrated at birth into recognizable configurations that later in life will become meaningful social cues.

The second issue regarding these early expressions relates to individual differences between newborns. Any individual differences in facial neuromuscular integration from the beginning may help stamp the nature of ensuing relationships. A singular study bears on this point.[10] Bennett carefully watched the routine morning activities of newborn nursery nurses and their charges. He noted that most infants were quickly character-typed by the nurses, who rapidly and fairly unanimously dubbed one infant as a lover boy, naughty but lovable, and another as a "simple nice girl, not sexy or flirtatious," and so on. The nature of the nurses' interplay with each infant was strongly colored by how they saw his or her personality.

Even if these observations are a simple case of "adultomorphizing" on the nurses' part (an important event in itself because it is so ubiquitous), the nurses' fantasies are not woven out of whole cloth. What are the individual cues that provide the seeds of the fantasies? Bennett remarks on differences in each infant related to rhythms of wakefulness, arousal, and alertness. He also stressed attention to differences in facial expression during alertness as an important cue for this common kind of early personality typing.

The smile. During the first two weeks of life smiles are seen during dreaming sleep (also called irregular or rapid eye movement—REM sleep) and during drowsiness. They are rarely seen when the infant is awake and alert with his eyes open. Some of these smiles are fleeting, some prolonged, some are asymmetrical and quite wry-looking, where only one corner of the mouth goes up, and others are beatific. They appear to bear no relationship to anything going on in the external world and are solely the reflection of cycles of neurophysiological excitation and discharges within the brain, unrelated to gas bubbles or any other part of the body except the brain's intrinsic activity. It has been called endogenous smiling because of its internal origin and its unrelatedness to anything external.[11] They have also been called reflexive.

At sometime between six weeks and three months, depending on the study, the smile becomes exogenous, elicited by external events. Different sights and sounds will now reliably elicit a smile. However, among all the external stimuli once again it is the stimuli of a human face, the human gaze, a high-pitched voice, and tickling which are now the most predictable elicitors of the smile. Thus, in becoming exogenous, the smile becomes predominantly a social smile. Still the morphology of the smile does not change, although what triggers it does.

Beginning around the third month, the smile takes another developmental leap and becomes an instrumental behavior. By instrumental we mean simply that the infant will now produce the smile in order to get a response from someone, such as a return smile from mother or a word from her. The smile itself, however, still looks the same.

The last developmental advance is that around the fourth month the smile comes under sufficiently smooth and coordinated performance that it can begin to be performed simultaneously along with a part or parts of other facial expressions; more complex expressions emerge, such as a smile performed with a slight frown. More study is needed here to determine when expressions from different motivational patterns begin to integrate to form more complex and often ambivalent expressions.

These stages in the development in the smile would be impossible without the parallel advances in the infant's perceptual and cognitive abilities that permit the same old smile to appear under different conditions, in response to different stimuli, and in the service of different functions.

Why do we believe these transformations to be largely the unfolding of innate tendencies? The remarkable similarity in course and timetable for infants raised in very different environmental and social conditions lends some weight to the argument. Even more convincing are the studies of blind children who have had no visual opportunity to see or imitate smiles or receive visual reinforcement or feedback for their smiles. Until four to six months their smiles are relatively normal compared to sighted children and follow the same developmental stages and timetable. However, beginning around the fourth to sixth month the blind children begin to show a dampening or muting of facial expressiveness in general, so that the display of their smiles is less dazzling and captivating. This suggests that after an initial epoch of the unfolding of innate tendencies (under the impact of average experiences), some visual feedback or reinforcement appears to be necessary to maintain the fullest range of display of the smile behavior.

To summarize this developmental history: the smile moves from a reflexive activity (internally triggered) to a social response (externally elicited by human and other stimulation) to an instrumental behavior (produced to elicit social responses from others) to a sufficiently coordinated behavior to combine with other facial expressions. This general course, though probably the most common for facial expressions, is certainly not the same for all expressive behaviors. Unlike the smile, the laugh is not present at birth and does not appear to go through an endogenous phase. It appears first as a response to external stimuli somewhere between the fourth and eighth month. At first, from four to six months it is most easily elicited by tactile stimulation, such as tickling. From seven to nine months auditory events become more effective, and from ten to twelve months it is most readily triggered by visual events.[12] Still like the smile, its form changes little from its first appearance throughout the rest of life. It is present in the blind and has been reported in feral children brought up by animals. Early on, it too becomes an instrumental behavior.

Displeasure. The cry face, with or without a cry, is the most dramatic and unequivocal expression of displeasure. The cry face, however, should be considered an end-point behavior, the last step, so to speak, in a patterned sequence of distinct facial expressions denoting increasing displeasure. The entire sequence of progressing expressions is roughly: first the face "sobers"; then a frown begins to form and deepens as the brows knit more; then the eyes begin to close partially as the upper cheeks raise and become flushed; the lower lip quivers and then the lips are retracted (pulled back) as the mouth opens; next the corners of the mouth turn down and the full cry face is achieved. Fuss noises may occur early on in the sequence, but it is only toward the end that the characteristic catches in breathing occur and the actual cry bursts out along with the cry face. The infant can, of course, stop at any point along the way within this sequence. The degree of displeasure will be interpreted from how far along in the patterned sequence he went. Several points along the way correspond to separate recognizable facial expressions: sobering, frowning, grimacing.

Each of these separate expressions, as well as the entire patterned sequence, follows a developmental course similar to that of the smile. These expressions are present at birth as reflexive activities, especially during sleep, and change very little in morphology throughout our lives. They become exogenous, externally elicited, behaviors earlier than the smile, and some observers believe that the instrumental use of the cry can be seen as early as three weeks of age. In any event, by the third month of life each of these expressions and the entire sequence to which they belong are ready and working as social and instrumental behaviors to help the infant conduct and regulate his half of the interaction with mother.

PULLING THINGS TOGETHER

I have discussed gazing, head movements, and facial expressions separately. Though we can write about or study each of these behaviors separately, in real life they belong together and are generally performed together. What is more, their simultaneous performance is integrated into behavioral "packages." These packages are the units of ongoing behavior which function as communicative units. For instance, in response to a disturbing stimulus, an infant may simultaneously break gaze and, while averting his face to the side, frown and grimace and emit a fuss sound. The simultaneous performance of these five behaviors is not something that the infant has to learn to coordinate. Instead, the particular integration itself is innately organized and reflects the unfolding of inborn tendencies toward organized actions. In ethological terms, each of the five separate behaviors can be considered an innate motor pattern. Similarly, their integrated performance can be considered an innate motor pattern of a higher order.

An example from the more complex realm of delight may help to fill in this notion. When we talk of a captivating infant smile, it is probable that much more is going on than just a full smile. The infant moves his head forward and tilts up his face, but without breaking gaze, as if he is trying to lift his head and face toward the person who elicited the smile. At the same time, body tension will noticeably increase as may limb movements, which may include a poorly coordinated effort to reach toward the person with his arms. The hands will open and close rhythmically. A gurgle may accompany these other acts. Once again, this entire specific integration of behaviors is unlearned.

There are three points to be made about these packages or units of ongoing behavior. The first I have already made, that

these integrated units are as innately determined as their component parts are, and they undergo a developmental course
mainly influenced by innate tendencies and organizational
changes with only a small contribution from processes of learning.

The second point is that these packages appear to operate as
functional units of communication within the flow of ongoing
behavior. These integrated innate motor patterns are for the
mother (or any average adult) the crucial stimulus which, once
received and processed, lead her to act in a specific way. In
animals, we would call the integrated infant behaviors innate
releasers. Referring back to the smile, if the same smile were performed with the same increase in body tension and limb movement, but without the attempted head raising and face tilting and
arm reaching, the impact of the communication would be significantly different. The adult would have inferred the same
thorough delight on the infant's part, but the infant would have
been viewed as a passive observer rather than as an active being
moving toward the source of the delightful stimulation. The
point, of course, is that the specific configuration of the integrated package of behaviors is perceived as a gestalt and is
understood as such. We do not yet know to what extent mothers
or other adults are themselves predisposed innately to perceive,
comprehend, and react to these packages. The majority of our
research has focused on the potency of the separate elements
rather than on their action as an integrated whole.

The third point about these integrated units of behavior is that
they may also be units in larger sequences that make up the
major motivational themes of approach, pleasure, avoidance,
and so on. The progression of units of ongoing behavior we have
seen, from face sobering through several progressing units to the
full cry face, described the displeasure behavioral pattern. We
assume that these sequential patterns, as well as the series of
units that make them up, are also largely determined by innate
factors.

Very clearly then, by three months at least, the infant is well
equipped with a large repertoire of behaviors to engage and
disengage his caregivers. All of his behaviors—the simple motor
patterns; the more complex combinations of these simple
patterns into integrated units; and the patterned sequences of

these units—have a strong innate predisposition. In addition, they have also been subject to the shaping process of learning during the early months of their emergence.

By the time we observe this very social infant toward the latter part of his first half year, his social capabilities are indeed formidable. He is fully ready to engage in that first phase of learning about and interacting with the human world. During these first six months he and his mother, utilizing their separate repertoires of behavior, have evolved their own interactive style and their own interactive fit as a pair.

4 / From Laboratory to Real Life

In the last chapter we were concerned with the infant in his first phase of learning about the human world. Earlier we discussed the behaviors that the mother has available to create a human stimulus world for the infant during this period. How does the interaction of these separate infant and mother behaviors function and result in such phenomena as interest, delight, boredom, and a relationship? How do the separate units of each partner's behavior fall into the patterned moves that create the choreography between them?

To answer these questions we will consider several experimental findings and hypotheses that provide ways of thinking about interactive patterns. Many of the findings have been generated in the laboratory or at least in experimentally manipulated situations. Compared to the mainly naturalistic observations I have heavily relied on up to this point, the experimental situation gives the scientist both freedom and control. He has the freedom to reach beyond the fairly disorderly series of events that natural situations offer up and to create new or non-natural events or situations that may critically test different hypotheses and generate broader generalizations. However, one disadvantage of the experimental approach is that many of the findings with potentially important implications for the care-giver-infant interaction appear too far removed from the natural situation as it is known to most mothers and clinicians to be transposable and useful.

The task of relating events from the laboratory to the natural situation will be easier if we keep it in mind that, even though the average mother-infant interaction is extremely chaotic compared to experimental events, whatever a mother does naturally can and must be considered a stimulus event for her infant or a response to him, and vice-versa, little different from any of the stimuli or responses encountered in the laboratory. Mother and infant behaviors are, after all, stimuli with different parameters such as intensity, complexity, or novelty. They also last a certain amount of time (they have a duration of presentation), with pauses in between (intertrial or interstimulus intervals). It is often necessary to get mechanistic in order to reemerge with a larger holistic point of view. That is the purpose of this chapter.

THE INFANT IS AN ACTIVE STIMULUS SEEKER

Today this statement is neither startling nor controversial. In fact, it has become an accepted and important starting point for thinking about what infants do. Most of the earlier theories ran counter to this notion. The infant was viewed as either needing protection from external stimuli or at best as a passive recipient of stimulation. Freud's speculations, which have been of far-reaching influence, were along these general lines, but with some provocative additional hypotheses. He speculated that simulation was accompanied by the build-up of excitation, which was experienced as unpleasure, while the discharge of this excitation was experienced as pleasurable. Later we shall come back to this notion. For the moment, however, doing it some injustice, we can let it stand as representative of the earlier hypotheses that the infant does not actively and pleasurably seek stimulation.

Over the past several decades, evidence has accumulated from many diverse areas that the infant, from birth, will seek out stimulation and even work for it. In fact, the seeking of stimulation has by now achieved the status of a drive or motivational tendency not unlike that of hunger, an analogy that is not far-fetched. Just as food is needed for the body to grow, stimulation is needed to provide the brain with the "raw materials" required for the maturation of perceptual, cognitive, and sensori-motor processes. The infant is provided with the tendencies to look for and get this needed "brain food."

We must distinguish two different types of stimulation that the infant seeks out, sensory or perceptual stimulation and intellectual or cognitive stimulation. Sensory stimulation would consist, for example, of the loudness or pitch of a sound or the intensity or complexity of a visual image. Cognitive stimuli, on the other hand, are stimulating because their contents bear some relationship to a referent stimulus (such as an image of the expected stimulus). The evaluation of the relationship between the stimulus and its referent is what sets into motion various mental operations and processes. For instance, if an infant heard a loud noise many times in a row, and then heard a quieter one, the quieter noise would provide him with less sensory stimulation, since it has less intensity. However, the quieter noise would provide him with an increase in cognitive stimulation, since he would immediately evaluate and compare the new stimulus to the previous one. The relationship of the stimulus to a referent, rather than the properties of the stimulus itself, would constitute the cognitive stimulation, the engagement and working of the mental faculties. The distinction is not always quite clear. Some stimulation, especially very early in life, could be construed as solely perceptual or sensory. However, all cognitive stimuli have to be received through perceptual processes to get into the brain and accordingly must produce some perceptual stimulation even though the cognitive stimulation may be the one of primary importance.

This distinction is of extreme importance to us because in a way it demarks the beginning of what can rightfully be called intellectual activity. By around three months of age, the cognitive stimulation provided by many caregiver stimulus events starts to become the more predominant. The infant is becoming more of a cognitive than a sensory animal, though he never stops being a sensory animal too. there is, however, no sharp change at three months; the shift is quite gradual.

It is perhaps not surprising that the young infant should seek out and need stimuli to set in motion the maturation of his perceptual and sensory processes. It is more surprising to find that our explanations of infant behavior reguire that we view the infants as utilizing cognitive operations from the first weeks of life. In Piaget's terms, the infant from the beginning is an active agent in expending mental work in the process of "effortful assimilation" of environmental stimuli to form internal schema of his external world. Jerome Bruner has recently stressed this idea in stating that a central tendency of the infant's mental life is the "active process of hypothesis formation and hypothesis testing."[1] Active stimulus seeking is certainly a precursor of curiosity, that powerful tendency which more and more is viewed as a force crucial for adaptation and survival in man and in other animals.

Still, though the infant is certainly a stimulus seeker, his quest for stimuli is not indiscriminate or without built-in safeguards. He will avoid being inundated by excessive stimulation and will also avoid being immobilized by having to attend and respond to all environmental events no matter how trivial or boring.

STIMULATION AND ATTENTION

The level of stimulation. The findings of many diverse researchers all point toward the same general relationship between infant attention and the level of stimulation.[2] If the level of stimulation is too low, even though he is aware of its presence, he will barely attend to it, or if he does he will quickly lose interest. If the level of stimulation is too high, he will avoid it by turning away or crying (for help to get someone else to remove it). When the level of stimulation is more moderate, somewhere between the two extremes, his attention will be more easily captured and maintained. Within the moderate range, as the strength of the stimulus increases the infant's attention is maintained longer, or he attends more frequently, up to some optimal point when the stimulus level is becoming too high and his attention falls off. This situation is illustrated in Figure 2.

This general tendency applies to the strength or quantity of all of the various parameters that make up a stimulus: its intensity, or complexity, or amount of contrast, or rate of change, or degree of novelty. It also applies to stimuli in all modalities: visual, auditory, tactile, kinesthetic. It is a fairly broad generalization. Each particular parameter in each stimulus modality and at different ages will have its own particular curve. The curve may peak more toward the lower or higher end, and it may be steeper or flatter. Furthermore, the position on the scale and its shape will have its own developmental course for each of these stimulus elements. For instance, what may be a moderate level of complexity in a visual image that maintains the attention of a

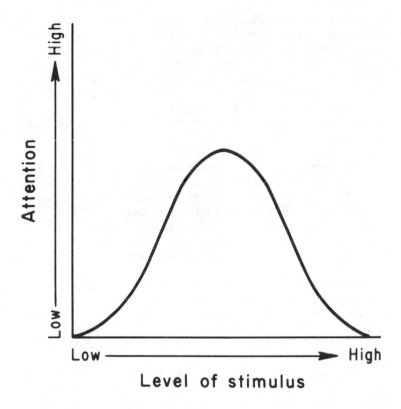

2. *The relationship between the level of attention and the level of stimulation.*

one-month-old may be at too low a level to hold the attention of a three-month-old. At the same time, what is considered a moderate level of light intensity from the same image may not have changed from one to three months.

Our generalization covers the individual cases and their histories provided by different stimulus parameters on different modalities. In fact, we should at this point go back and relabel Figure 1. On the abscissa, instead of just indicating a general level of stimulation from low to high, we can separate and specify the stimulus parameter: intensity, degree of contrast, complexity, and so on, and draw a series of curves for each. In fact, to have more complete knowledge in this situation we should have the developmental curves of all the important (to the infant) stimulus parameters in all modalities.

There is, however, one serious problem. The generalization and its illustration in the theoretical curve drawn in the figure do not, in fact, correspond to what we really observe. Actual observations of infants responding to increasing levels of stimulation strongly suggest that when some upper threshold level of stimulation is exceeded, the infant "turns off" rapidly. He suddenly averts gaze, turns his face away rapidly, and may also withdraw sharply. Accordingly, the gradual fall off of inattention as the stimulus level approaches the highest end is not seen. Instead, there is a precipitous fall in attention whenever some threshold of tolerance is passed. It is as if the infant will not or cannot tolerate stimulation beyond this point and shuts off his processes of attention. This is illustrated in Figure 3.

Repetitious stimulation. So far we have been discussing changing levels of stimulation and attention. What about the many repeating sounds and sights that fill our daily life or that of an infant? This large territory of events includes the category of stimuli we call background stimulus events. Although we "want" the infant to be highly responsive to the environment (or the caregiver), we also want that responsivity to be somewhat selective. We do not want him to be so stimulus-bound that he remains constantly highly responsive to the background trivia of life—the ticking of clocks, or the noise of each passing car. He must have some way to tune out the background noise while maintaining an open sensitivity to new or altered or otherwise salient stimuli that come along.

The infant is provided with a means of accomplishing this. When the infant is presented with the same stimulus repeatedly, he will react to it less and less on each successive presentation. This is called habituation. More precisely, habituation is the progressive response decrement to a repeated unchanging stimulus. The fall off in response is not due to fatigue. Habituation is demonstrated in three-month-olds and forms of it are probably present at birth. It is most convincingly demonstrated to me each day on the New York subways where infants of all ages seem to

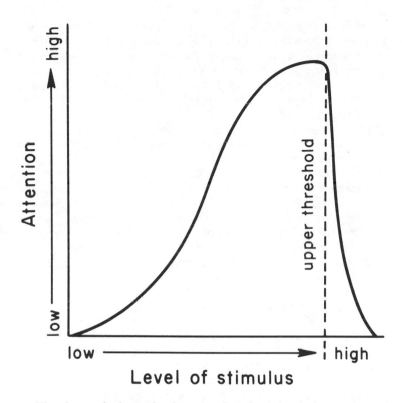

3. *The observed relationship between the infant's level of attention and the level of stimulation provided by a caregiver.*

be able to tune out the rhythmic roaring and lurching at stops and starts in order to stay asleep or maintain a remarkably even level of social attentiveness to whomever they are with.

I shall describe in some detail how an average habituation experiment is done. The flow of manipulated stimulus presentations provides an excellent point of comparison with, and reference for, the flow of infant-elicited maternal behaviors in naturally occurring interactions. In a visual habituation experiment, the infant is placed in an infant seat and shown a picture or image of something, for example, a bulls-eye pattern. This visual stimulus remains in view for usually about thirty seconds. The researcher counts the amount of time and the number of times the infant looks at the stimulus target during its thirty seconds of presentation. (In addition to measuring the amount of visual attention, the researcher can also observe and record other behaviors, such as facial expressions and body movements, or he can also record changes in heartrate and other physiological changes.)

The bulls-eye pattern is then turned off or taken away for an "intertrial interval" of again about thirty seconds. The same bulls-eye pattern is then re-presented for another thirty-second period, the infant's response again recorded, and so on. This procedure is repeated for six or so times. With each repeat, the infant's attention wanes and he looks less and less. However, on the seventh presentation a new stimulus is shown, say a checkerboard pattern instead of the old bulls-eye. The infant's interest is immediately revived by the new stimulus, and his level of attention is generally as high as on the first presentation of the first stimulus.

The introduction of the second stimulus into the experiment is important because it proves that the infant has not lost his ability to respond because of fatigue or some other process indicating neurological loss of ability. He has simply become "bored" with the repetition of the same old thing. Figure 4, schematically adapted from Kagan and Lewis,[3] shows the decreasing time spent attending to the progressive six presentation of the first stimulus (S_1) and the time spent attending to the new stimulus (S_2) on the seventh presentation.

The implications of these simple experiments are far-reaching and crucial for our understanding of what is effective stimulation within the mother-infant relationship and how interest can be captured and maintained in the infant's daily life. For the infant to get bored, he has to "know" or "remember" in some fashion, over a thirty-second interval, the nature of the stimulus. Otherwise, he could not have an "Oh, that again" response, as Lewis has described it. The second point is that for any stimulus to "work," to be interesting, it cannot be repeated over and over. A mother cannot do the exact same thing six times in a row and get away with it. The stimulus events that are her behavior must almost constantly be modified to maintain the same level of attention. She has to change to stay in the same place.

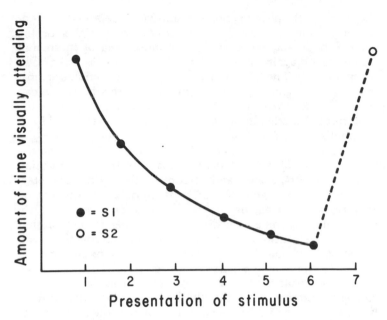

4. *The progressive decrease in visual attention upon repeated presentations of the same stimulus (S1), and the "rebound" in visual attention when a new stimulus (S2) is presented.*

From sensory to cognitive stimulation. So far we have discussed mainly the effects of stimulation on the infant's perceptual and sensory processes, as they are reflected through attention. At some point in development, certainly by three months, the infant has begun to engage, evaluate, and cognitively deal with the specific content of a stimulus. The quantity of the stimulation or of any of its physical parameters will no longer be as telling as the relationship between the significant content of the stimulus and some other referent. For example, the stimulus power of a face to hold attention will no longer reside in the degree of complexity, light and dark contrast, amount of angularity, the sum of all of the stimuli that happen to be a face, but rather in the contrastive or similar relationship between that present face and the internal schema of a known or expected face.

In this shift, the phenomenon of habituation represents a mid-way point. One can assume that after several sights of the stimulus the infant begins to form some schema of it, so that when he sees it again, thirty seconds later, he can act like "Oh, that again" only if he is forming a schema of the stimulus against which he is comparing the next stimulus. If this is so, we can begin to speak of the stimulation as coming not only from the properties of the stimulus itself but also from its relationship to the infant's schema.

Much recent evidence supports the notion that it is around the third month of life, if not before, that the infant is forming schema of objects, events, and persons in his world. This internal mental "picture" gives him an expectation as to how a thing should look, or smell, or sound. If the infant encounters an object that is in some way different from his picture of that object—an element of novelty has been introduced—there will now exist a mismatch between the actual stimulus and its schema. The amount of mismatch can be usefully labeled the degree of discrepancy.[4] It is as if the infant tries to figure out whether the present object is really the same as or different from his expectation of it. The source of stimulation now resides mainly in the stimulus-schema mismatch rather than in any physical properties of the stimulus itself. It is only a short step to see how the continual operation of match-mismatch evaluations of stimuli will enhance the establishment of schema and continually enlarge their scope.

Since now the degree of discrepancy itself has become the source of stimulation which generates and maintains attention, Kagan and others go a step further and state that there must be some predictable relationships between the degree of discrepancy (cognitive stimulation) and attention. The relationship we saw between the level of perceptual stimulation and attention (Figure 3) is essentially similar to the relationship between the level of cognitive stimulation (degree of discrepancy) and attention. Very slight degrees of discrepancy provide very slight stimulation and produce low levels of attention. Increasing degrees of discrepancy produce progressively more attention up to some maximum threshold beyond which the infant finds the experience unpleasant and avoids it. When the threshold is greatly exceeded, we assume that the discrepancy between that stimulus and the schema for it has been stretched well beyond the breaking point. The infant thus can not see the stimulus as even related to his working schema for what was expected. He thus has no reason to perform a match-mismatch evaluation and treats the overly discrepant stimulus as an entirely novel object. His attention may thus flag after the tolerance point was exceeded.

EXCITEMENT

Terms. "Excitement" goes by several other names and concepts in the current scientific literature. Activation, arousal, and tension are the most prevalent. Each carries its own historical baggage, theoretical viewpoints, and heuristic value. I have chosen to use the term excitement for several reasons. First of all, there is currently much reevaluation of the nature of these terms, the phenomena they refer to, and their value as useful working concepts.[5] Accordingly, at this time no single term captures the consensus of current thinking as it applies to infants. Nonetheless, they all refer to a crucially needed concept about the internal state of the infant, a concept that directs itself to the dimension of the intensity and level of activity of internal processes reflected in overt behavior and presumably in the infant's subjective experience. The more colloquial term excitement quite readily captures everyone's common experience of the overt behaviors and subjective sensations that accompany internal neurological and neurophysiological processes.

Excitement and attention. Fluctuations in the level of excitement can be caused by internal or external events. During sleep, when we can assume there is no appreciable external stimulation, the infant and adult go through rhythmic shifts in their internal state. In dreaming sleep, there is selective activity, producing endogenous smiles and other facial expressions, and irregularities in physiological activities such as heartrate and breathing. During deep sleep, there is slower, more regular body activity. These regular shifts reflect the rhythmic changes in the discharge patterns and activity of the brain. This kind of fluctuation in excitement requires no processes of attention whatsoever. It all comes from within.

During the first several weeks of life the baby's situation is somewhat similar to sleep even when he is awake. He shifts from drowsiness to alert inactivity, to alert activity, and occasionally to the fuss-cry state. Each of these waking states, like the sleeping states, is largely determined by the ongoing periodic shifts in the intrinsic discharge patterns of the brain. Each also represents a different point along an excitation dimension.

But external events are no longer irrelevant and attention becomes increasingly important. Even though the cycle of these waking states is still largely driven by intrinsic brain activities, external stimuli can prolong or terminate a state or certainly drive the baby into a higher state, such as the fuss-cry state or bring him "down," helping to lull him into drowsiness. The infant's ability to attend to external stimuli begins to play more of a role, though still a secondary one, in determining his internal state of excitement. This is particularly true during the state called "alert inactivity," when the infant is visually alert but not moving his body and limbs about. During alert inactivity the infant is most attentive to and receptive toward external stimulation. He spends more time looking at and pursuing visual objects and attending to sounds. In a sense his ability to attend is greatly influenced by the level and pattern of intrinsic brain excitation, by the "state" he is in. Attention at this point in development is the handmaiden of intrinsic brain excitation. Still the handmaiden is not without some power. Within limits, for example, given that the infant is already in the alert inactive state, whatever external stimulation is attended to will influence the infant's level of excitement.

By the time the third month of life has arrived, the situation has long been equalized or even reversed. Now within certain limits, the level of excitation is largely influenced by the infant's attention. The infant is now capable of maintaining a fairly constant internal state which allows him to be attentive and responsive to the environment for fairly long stretches at a time, certainly up to fifteen minutes and often much longer. It is during these stretches that most playful social interactions occur. At such times, his level of excitement will be mainly influenced by incoming stimulation. This perceptual input is largely determined by his attention processes, which cannot be separated from the regulation of internal neurophysiological state or excitement.[6] The infant's control of his attention gives him control over stimulus input and thereby control over internal excitement. This is especially true for visual stimuli, as we have seen. His ability to regulate or gate the perceptual input in other modalities is less complete. (How and to what extent an infant can tune out auditory, tactile, and kinesthetic stimuli is a fascinating question we shall return to later.)

Excitement and stimulation. The general relationship described between stimulation and attention applies to much of the relationship between stimulation and excitation. Low levels of stimulation produce low levels of excitement. As the level of stimulation increases, so will the degree of excitement. However, at high levels of stimulation, attention can be turned off, in some modalities at least, shutting off the incoming stimulation and allowing the degree of excitement to subside. In these situations attention can be diverted instantaneously. Excitement, however, acts as if it had more momentum and requires a longer period to decrease. It also requires a longer time to build up. During the orienting response when attention is first captured, the level of excitement is probably nil until well after an internal "evaluation" of the new stimulus is over. At the very high levels where overstimulation is clearly in effect, the level of excitement can climb to a point where the not uncommon situation of uncontrollable crying, wailing, and flailing of the limbs occurs and goes on for some time. Excitement at this level appears to have no self-regulating mechanism to turn itself off except through fatigue.

In this realm of excitement the distinctions between sensory and cognitive stimuli become subtle. Tickling provides a good example. The more vigorous and dynamic the tickling, the higher goes the infant's excitement. The stimulus can clearly be classified as sensory. However, several months later the excitement begins to come from the surprise of knowing or not knowing exactly when the burst of tickling will strike. This evolves into an entire game with many variants where two different stimuli are operating simultaneously to heighten the excitement. There is the excitement generated by the sensory stimulation of the tickle itself, and on top of that there is the excitement generated by the cognitive stimulation of creating expectancies and violating them (causing surprise).

Affect. The development of affect or emotion has both intrigued and partially eluded the understanding of students of human behavior. Part of the problem is that the most crucial aspect of an affect is its subjective feeling of joy or displeasure or whatever, and subjective feelings cannot be observed or even directly tapped in a nonverbal infant. They can only be inferred from overt behaviors which, although reflective of the feeling state, are at least one step away.

Given this state of affairs, most of the studies of affect have been observational or experimental studies of the overt behaviors that reflect and communicate the subjective state, or studies of a more philosophical and metapsychological nature dealing with the subjective aspects of affects. The problem is still with us. Still it is strange that our pursuit and understanding of human perception, cognition, and motor skills have so outstripped our understanding of affect. Life without affect is as unthinkable as life without cognition. In addition, psychiatric disturbances, what we consider abnormal behavior, are almost invariably manifested by disturbances in affect, certainly as much as by disturbances in cognition or perception. It is only quite recently, however, that there has been a concerted return of interest and inquiry to this vital area.

Freud's major explanation of affect will serve as the first piece in putting together this unfinished puzzle. He proposed that all stimulation caused internal tension or excitement which was invariably experienced as unpleasure. The infant then sought to discharge the tension, and the tension reduction was accompanied by the experience of pleasure. There are several problems with Freud's model. First of all, infants actively seek stimulation, and, second, the build-up of excitement clearly can be pleasurable. Freud also postulated that a quantum of stimulus energy which entered the system was converted to a quantum of tension energy which had to be discharged. We now know that stimulation does not act like a quantum of energy that has got into a closed system where it presses for discharge to maintain equilibrium. The infant tolerates and thrives on more and more stimu-

lation as he matures. Lastly, the cessation of pleasurable stimulation can be experienced as aversive.

At first glance it appears that we have entirely dismantled
Freud's model, but this is not so. What remains is a kernal concept: affect is related to the build-up and fall-off of stimulation
and tension. Freud took an extreme position in stating that the
build-up side was solely unpleasurable and the fall-off side
purely pleasurable. Sroufe ties together four diverse instances of
a rise and fall in stimulation and excitement. The first instance is
taken from the dreaming (REM) sleep of neonates. The work of
Emde and others suggests that during REM sleep, the more primitive subcortical portions of the brain rhythmically discharge,
creating rising and falling cycles of neurological excitation. The
endogenous smile of the dreaming neonate occurs when the level
of excitation rises above and then falls below a postulated
threshold. The second instance deals with the awake organism in
the presence of external rather than internal stimuli. Berlyne
proposes that an "arousal jag," a sudden increase and decrease in
the ongoing level of excitement, is required to produce an affective experience.[7] The third instance involves an infant exposed to
the cognitive stimulation of a stimulus-schema mismatch. Kagan
proposes that while the infant is processing and working on the
incongruity, tension will mount until he has assimilated the
stimulus, that is, solved the problem, at which point the tension
dissipates, manifested behaviorally in a smile.[8] The fourth instance comes from Sroufe's studies of laughter in infants. He
finds that for a sound to make an infant laugh it must produce a
sharp "tension fluctuation." Furthermore, the most successful
form of sound stimulation to produce this rapid fluctuation was
a stimulus that accelerated in intensity to an abrupt cutoff. A
steep gradient of tension and rapid recovery were best to produce laughter.

The question still remains whether pleasure or unpleasure
resides, so to speak, solely on the uphill or downhill side of the
excitement jag. Freud is definite that tension build-up is aversive
and only tension reduction is pleasurable. Kagan suggests that
for cognitive stimuli the build-up is slightly negative or uncertain
in affect tone, and the decrease in tension produced by successful
assimilation is affectively positive while the decrease in tension
produced by a failure of assimilation and stimulus avoidance is

affectively negative. Sroufe occupies the least committed position, maintaining that the build-up of excitement can be either positively or negatively affectively toned or neutral, depending on the ongoing conditions and context in which the stimulation occurs. Similarly the excitement-reduction phase can be positively or negatively toned in affect, again depending on the nature of the infant's engagement with the stimulus and the context of that engagement.

By some set of criteria any activity that is maintained or repeated can be considered pleasurable. During the build-up phase the fact that the infant finds the stimulus attention-maintaining, which in fact allows the excitement to mount, argues that the build-up phase is pleasurable even if not sufficiently so to produce smiles and laughter. This is a roundabout way of saying that, if you need a steep gradient of build-up and fall-off, the stimuli causing the build-up have to be able to capture and hold the infant's attention.

I have so far begged the question of what determines the direction of affect. Which pattern or sequence of phenomena will cause joy and which unhappiness? We simply don't always know. Clearly stimuli that are too intense or too incongruous, or in any way build up too rapidly or with too high a fluctuation, will be experienced as aversive. Still the onset of a stimulation, say a tickle or song, of "ideal" intensity and "perfect" rate of build-up could result in a beaming or a screaming baby depending on complex factors that are not fully clear to us yet. Certainly they include the infant's state and affective tone and the direction of their trend at the moment of stimulation, the situation and context, including the history of past such events, and the state of other rhythmic systems such as hunger and wakefulness. Affect still remains a partial mystery, but at least we begin to see its relation to stimulation, attention, and excitement.

THE STIMULUS WORLD OF THE HOME

One of the major differences between most laboratory and most home stimuli is that home stimulation as provided by caregivers is far more heterogeneous and variable. At home the interactive stimuli are almost exclusively the mother and her behavior. The mother's face or voice or body is almost constantly changing and the changes are often dramatic. Because of this, it is difficult to talk about *the* stimulus level of any "face" or sound or behavior she performs since the stimulus level changes during the very performance of the behavior. Nonetheless, the generalization we have learned from examining the more static or constant laboratory stimuli will stand us in good stead in understanding the highly variable events the mother provides. The reality we are confronted with is that almost all infant-elicited social behaviors are highly dynamic. That is both our problem and their advantage. To conceptualize the effect on attention or excitement of a fluctuating stimulus, we have to examine how the level of that stimulus changes over time. Almost any infant-elicited social behavior provides an adequate example. We can start with the mock-surprise expression. The rising and falling stimulus intensity over time of a mock-surprise expression can be represented diagrammatically as shown in Figure 5, which shows the waxing and waning of the fullness of display as distributed in time.

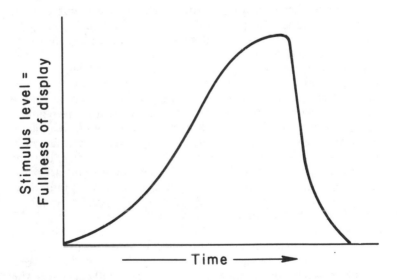

5. *The manner in which the stimulus level, consisting of the fullness of display of a behavior, can change over the duration of its performance.*

The fullness of display at any moment during the performance of the expression corresponds in the laboratory situation to the intensity of stimulation. If instead of a visual stimulus we had taken an infant-elicited vocalization such as "hiiiiiiya," we could draw a similar curve where the shape reflects changes in both loudness and pitch. When we view the mother's behavior in this way, the same generalizations governing the relationship between the stimulus level (perceptual or cognitive) and the level of attention and of excitement apply just as they did in the laboratory. As the level of stimulation increases and decreases within each stimulus event, in the course of such a maternal behavior, so will the infant's attention and excitement.

Whereas each stimulus event has its own local history, that event and its local history do not occur in a vacuum or out of relation to the larger history of previously occurring events. We must consider for a series of such events the trends in the level of stimulation and in the level of excitement. Here too there are upper thresholds of tolerance. A stimulus burst that was tolerable, in fact fascinating, when it occurred against a lower background level of excitement might be intolerable if it occurred against a background level that had drifted higher, since then it might "push" the degree of excitement beyond some upper threshold.

Now that we have reintroduced the element of time, by having to consider how a mother actually modulates the stimulus level of a behavior over the duration of its performance, we are in a better position to see how she can generate and regulate affect in the infant. We can redraw Figure 5 showing two different ways a mother can modulate the fullness of display of a mock-surprise expression (Figure 6). In curve number 2, but not number 1, we recognize the steep gradient of a rapid acceleration, abrupt cut-off, and fall-off of the level of stimulation. While curve number 2 might result in a smile, curve number 1 would be quite attention-maintaining.

The mother's enormous flexibility in her capacity to perform infant-elicited behaviors with different distribution in time provides her with potentially exquisite control over the infant's attention, excitement, and affect. I say potentially, because the infant has a great deal to say about it.

A second major difference between experimental and home

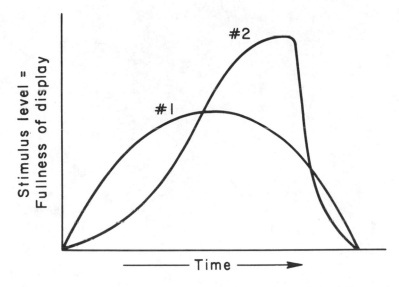

6. *Two ways in which the stimulus level, consisting of the fullness of display of a behavior, can change over the duration of its performance.*

stimulation concerns how we define the unit we call a stimulus (descriptively or functionally). In the experimental situation the task is relatively easy, as we have seen. Since it is a predefined entity, it can be a very complex series of events as well as a simple one. In the home, with a naturally behaving mother, the task is not at all easy. The unit of stimulation that we are interested in is often a hodgepodge of different stimulus events where the first task is discovering that such a melange exists as a regular entity and acts as a stimulus. Once definable regularities in a mother's behavior have been identified as repeating units that act as stimuli, we find that the generalizations regarding habituation and the generation and violation of expectancies also apply to maternal behaviors as stimuli.

We can now return to the actual infant-caregiver interaction and explore its goals, structure, and functions against this background of current findings and theory.

5 / Where Do the Steps Lead?

The immediate goal of a face-to-face play interaction is to have fun, to interest and delight and be with one another. During these stretches of purely social play between mother and infant, there are no tasks to be accomplished, no feeding or changing or bathing on the immediate agenda. There is nothing even that has to be taught. In fact, if the task is to teach the infant something, he won't be able to learn what the play experience might hold for him. We are dealing with a human happening, conducted solely with interpersonal "moves," with no other end in mind than to be with and enjoy someone else.

There is no way to overstress the importance of such a seemingly effortless endeavor. We have all accepted in the main that the infant's first and prototypic caring and loving relationship is established with his primary caregiver. But what is a relationship and how does it become established? The infant first has to learn to be with someone and to create and share the experiences that a relationship is built on. Beside the gratification of feeding and warmth, these involve the mutual creation of shared pleasure, joy, interest, curiosity, thrills, awe, fright, boredom, laughter, surprise, delight, peaceful moments, silences resolving distress, and many other such elusive phenomena and experiences that make up the stuff of friendship and love.

Having fun can be considered the immediate goal of play for two reasons. First, if you ask mothers why they play with their infants, most will answer something like, "I don't know, we usually have fun." That, in fact, is her subjective experience and sense of the point or goal of the activity. The second reason is more conceptual and practical. Interest and delight also capture the observer's sense of what the activity is about. In addition, these words are readily translatable into the psychological terms and concepts we have been exploring: stimulation, attention, excitement, and affect. Once translated, interest and delight become more amenable to whatever experimental or theoretical maneuvers we need to perform in order to understand social play more fully.

By interest and delight I mean the mutual providing of stimulus events of such a nature that attention is engaged and maintained enough to allow for the build-up and fluctuation in excitement within a tolerable range so that affectively positive experiences are generated. That may be a roundabout way of talking about it, but such is the state of our science. Both partners must regulate the quality, quantity, and timing of stimulus events so that attention, excitement, and affect can rise and fall, each within its own optimal range.

As we have seen, to keep things within an optimal range, the stimulus events cannot be too weak, or too powerful, or too simple, or too complex, or too familiar, or too novel. Successive events cannot be too repetitive or attention is lost and excitement falls below the optimal range; affect becomes neutral. On the other hand, successive stimuli cannot be too drastically dissimilar or the infant will not be able to engage them cognitively. It sounds like a tight and narrow path requiring precise navigation conducted with conscious and careful reckoning each moment of the way. Fortunately, the opposite is closer to the truth. It requires a mother with no other thought in mind except to have fun with her baby and a baby in the mood to have fun.

We are, it turns out, extremely playful animals. We play with everything and anything, including our own behavior. We find it engrossing and amusing to play with our voices and faces and movements in the sense of experiencing pleasure in the creation of new variations, elaborations, and combinations of simple behaviors. Song, mime, and dance are most probably the cultural ritualizations of this process. A mother faced with a willing baby is placed in the almost irresistible position of being able to play with her baby by playing with her own behavior.

Fun, in the sense of joy in playing, is a key notion because it changes how we act and thus what may happen. A caregiver who is having fun by "playing" the natural instruments of her voice, face, head, and body and orchestrating them for, and in conjunction with, her baby will be affectively "alive." She will provide stimulation that corresponds more closely to the optimal range of stimulus events to which the infant is constitutionally preset to receive than does virtually any other source of stimuli in an average environment. If she is having fun, her behavior will consist of those infant-elicited social behaviors which are predesigned by the long course of evolution to be for the infant the best "sound-light show" on earth. If she is not having fun and faking it, or just going through the motions, the pair will have an "off" day, or the play session will be shorter than usual, or there will be no dance at all.

Once the baby is having fun, in the sense of experiencing his mother's behavior as interesting enough to capture his attention and shift his level of excitement within a range and time frame that produces pleasurable affective experiences, then he will manifest his interest and delight through smiles and coos and an alert avid gaze and face. The mother then experiences these displays as deeply gratifying and positively reinforcing. She will thus seek to maintain the infant at a level of attention and excitement wherein he will perform the affective displays which in turn produce in her those behaviors that maintain optimal levels of stimulation for him. A mutual feedback system is in operation. The mother tends to adjust the stimulus level of her behavior within the optimal range appropriate for the infant. They both thus tend toward the same goal of maintaining a set of optimal ranges, which correspond to the experiences of mutual interest and delight, of following one another in the dance pattern.

The notion of "optimal range" helps in thinking about the immediate goal of the interaction. Both partners can regulate the amount of effective stimulation impinging on the infant so that, if the ongoing level has shot above or fallen below some upper or lower thresholds, both partners have the behaviors at their disposal to bring the level back within the optimal range and to make the finer adjustments to keep it there. However, the notion of a fixed, rigid range which is the set-goal of a mutual feedback system certainly does not do justice to the flexibility and fluidity of the actual system shared by mother and infant. I have described it so far almost like a thermostat in the home which is set to turn the heat off when the temperature goes over 70 degrees and turn the heat back on when the temperature falls below 60 degrees. To take the analogy further, the mother and infant negotiate a system that allows them continually to change the absolute level and the width of the tolerance band of the agreed-upon range. Most play sessions go through periods of excitement and at times great hilarity and then pass into quiet, more restful stretches before the next up-and-down cycle begins. The exact course is not predictable and changes from day to day. In any event, this natural ebb and flow requires that the optimal range be, so to speak, a moving and changing target.

The next crucial issue is how the pair mutually agree about the momentary nature and position of the goal, and how each of them regulates their steps toward that goal. It is essential to emphasize that I am talking about the immediate or momentary goal of face-to-face play. This is a goal that allows us to ask such questions as, Why at this instant did the mother do this when right before the baby did that? The notion of a mutual feedback system allows us to conceptualize these kinds of questions.

At first glance, it seems out of perspective to consider play and having fun as occupying such a key role in the social interactions between mother and infant. Where do loving and needing to care for and identifying with the infant come into view? These are powerful motivating forces that mothers feel deep inside, but we have barely touched upon them and don't quite know how to. Certainly no face-to-face play would ever occur if a mother were not activated by these deeper forces and the long-range goals that accompany them. Still the question arises: If the mother does love and feels the need to care for and identify with her infant, and they are sitting across from each other face to face, what will happen? How will those motives translate into what acts? How do you love your baby so that a social interaction emerges? It is here that playing and having fun come into operation. They are an already available and ideally suited set of human operations to effect the translation from the longer-range motives into the behaviors that constitute the interaction and provide guidelines for the flow of the whole process.

THE VIRTUES OF "MESSING UP"

There is no such thing as an ideal caregiver who is exquisitely sensitive to all infant behaviors and who responds accordingly.

Such a person and such a situation are inconceivable because of the nature of social interactions. Both mother and infant, in attempting constantly to adjust their behavior to one another's, are in continual flux. The array of stimuli that the mother provides for the infant and the infant's level of attention, excitement, and affect repeatedly fall below some optimal level where interest is lost, and repeatedly climb above some optimal level where active aversion or termination is executed. In either case, both the mother and infant can readjust their behavior to bring the level temporarily back into an optimal range, where it fluctuates until the boundaries are again exceeded. That is the nature of a goal-correcting system. Much of play is spent crossing and recrossing the upper and lower boundaries, as well as within the optimal range.

The virtues of "messing up" are simple. By messing up, I mean that the mother, more consistently than usual, overshoots or undershoots the infant's tolerance boundaries. First of all, only when a boundary is exceeded is the infant forced to execute some coping or adaptive maneuver to correct or avoid the situation or to signal to the mother to alter the immediate stimulus environment. The infant behaviors, like any others, require constant practice, constant opportunities under slightly different conditions to become fully developed adaptive behaviors. Second, unless the mother frequently risks exceeding a boundary, whether by design or miscalculation, she will be unable to help stretch and expand the infant's growing range of tolerance for stimulation.

From this point of view, the mixture of off days, good days, bad moods, high moods, going through the motions, faking it, and overcompensating is all part of the necessary panorama of real events that help the infant acquire the interpersonal skills of coping with social interactions.

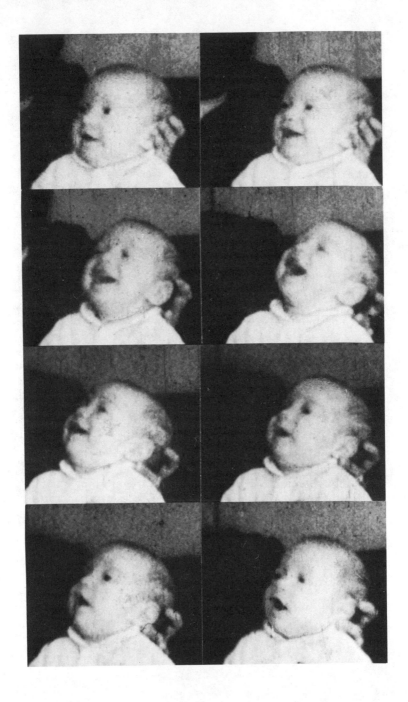

6 / Structure and Timing

A period of social interaction is the largest unit of activity we are concerned with. We usually call such periods play periods, because they essentially involve an early form of play restricted to the use of social behaviors. By a play period I mean simply a bounded period of time, anywhere from seconds to many minutes, when one or both members focus their attention on the *social* behaviors of the other partner and react to these behaviors with *social* behaviors of their own. During the first half year of life, these play interactions are different from later forms of play, in that they are accomplished without recourse to any toys or artifacts or game rules. The interplay is with interpersonal moves.

Given the unbelievably busy day of a mother (or any primary caregiver), there is not much time for play periods after all the inescapable functions of feeding, diapering, putting to bed, not to mention the activities unrelated to the baby. However, play periods do not require a specified slot in the day's schedule. They are periods that are taken or stolen or most usually spontaneously arise in the course of other activities and eclipse those activities for a while.

Some mothers schedule, so far as that is possible, their play periods on a fairly regular basis. Some find the infant most ready to play a few minutes before feedings. Other infants are too hungry and fussy then, but will play for minutes on end halfway or so through a feeding when the edge is off their hunger. Others play best after feeding and before sleep. Other pairs snatch periods of play from diapering or more often bathing sequences. Generally, mothers and infants will utilize any and all of these opportunities to indulge in a bout of play. For our purposes it doesn't matter much when a play period occurs. Once it has begun, all other ongoing external tasks come to a standstill and the focused interpersonal events that characterize social play take over and are essentially the same, no matter what was going on before or what will resume later.

It may seem strange that these play periods, which are of such crucial developmental importance, are not afforded the status of regularly structured activities, but rather are very often slipped in or burst forth unplanned in the course of other activities. Actually, because mutual play can only occur when the infant is awake and alert, which is a small portion of his day, a quite considerable part of his active time is spent in social play. Accordingly, even as an activity that may at times appear fleeting and infrequent, and stuck into the spaces between other activities, it occupies an impressive percentage of the infant's world experience. In fact, as we have seen, both the mother's and the infant's responsiveness to each other are predesigned to maximize the chances that this mutual activity will "take off" given the slightest excuse or, more accurately, given a wide range of adequate eliciting conditions.

THE PLAY PERIOD

Play periods invariably start with mother and infant catching one another's eye. There is then a moment of mutual gaze. What immediately follows this moment will determine whether or not a period of play will take off. If either mother or baby breaks gaze, for whatever reason, the play period is usually aborted, at least for the moment. If they hold gaze, then they both must signal to one another their readiness to engage in a social interaction. The mother signals with a version of the general facial display that involves eyebrow raising, eye widening, mouth opening, and head repositioning, such as in mock surprise. The infant on his side, especially as excitement mounts, performs his version of what appears to be similar behaviors. (These most probably derive with little change from the orienting response.) His eyes open wider, his eyebrows, to the extent he can control them, move uncertainly up and down, there is often mouth opening and smiling, and the head reorients to achieve a full-face position. This sometimes looks like a wagging of the head back and forth to "home in." Sometimes the head and neck strain forward in an approach movement. These movements and displays are the infant's corresponding signal of initiation to the mother. Once these signals have been exchanged and mutual gaze has held, the play period is off and running.

It is important to note that while all this is going on (it might have lasted as little as a second or so, since both displays are performed almost simultaneously), two other events essential to the play period were accomplished. First, during the exchange of "greeting" or signaling readiness, all other activities will have ceased and each partner will have captured the full attention of the other. Second, the very performance of the initiating behaviors brought about a reorientation so that both partners have come to a full-face position. Recall that in this position changes in facial expressions, gaze, and head movements will be most visible and potent as signals.

Of course not all play sessions start off with such a bang of mutual enthusiasm and simultaneous signaling of readiness. As often as not there are false starts, usually with the mother initiating and the infant refusing either to gaze or to greet. After several false starts the interaction may get going. They are often needed to arouse the baby to a sufficiently alert state to be able to interact.

The entire play period (if it is long enough) is subdivided into two smaller units that alternate: episodes of engagement, which are filled with the flow of social behaviors; and time-out episodes which have more the quality of rests and silences to readjust the interaction before engaging again.

An episode of engagement. An episode of engagement has the following features: It is a sequence of social behaviors of variable length bounded by clear pausing time on either side. The episode is generally ushered in with "greeting" behavior on the mother's part, less frequently on the infant's. In this way the onset of each episode of engagement is like the beginning of the play session, except that the greeting displays become less full and exaggerated. Nonetheless, some mothers will essentially regreet their infant at the start of each episode—which can happen as often as several times per minute. During an episode of engagement, the caregiver produces discrete behaviors, vocalizations or nonverbal behaviors or both, at a surprisingly regular rate, so that each episode has its own tempo. The regularity of tempo came as a surprise, perhaps in part because a mother can and does alter the degree of stress, or vigor, or amplitude of movements and sounds from moment to moment, thus giving the impression of changing tempo without actually doing so.

Each caregiver can alter the tempo from one engagement episode to the next and certainly has a wide range of characteristic tempos. It is interesting to speculate whether there are characteristic ranges for individuals, or cultures, or infant ages, and what may be the developmental consequences of such differences. The important point is that, for a given dyad, once a tempo is established for a particular episode it is generally maintained. The finding of a relatively regular rate of behavior during engagement episodes applies to vocal as well as nonvocal behaviors. The "addition" of sound to movement does not alter the tempo. Whether speaking or just moving, the caregiver provides the infant with discrete bursts of human behavior that come at roughly regular intervals. Accordingly, during each episode the infant is experiencing a sufficiently predictable stimulus world from which to form expectancies.

Much of human behavior has this characteristic of unfolding at rates that fluctuate, but only within certain limits at a predictable tempo. I have the impression that adults generally establish more regular behavioral tempos when interacting with infants as compared to other adults. In any event, an important aspect of the infant's stimulus world is the temporal patterning of that world. This applies to human behaviors as well as to all other stimulus events. It is probable that the range of tempos of caregivers' behaviors and the extent of momentary fluctuations in rate are well suited to the infant's temporal perceiving and processing structures. Our knowledge of an infant's attentional and cognitive processes would predict that a generally regular temporal process with limited but almost constant variability would be better suited for getting and holding his attention than a precisely fixed, completely redundant process or a completely unpredictable process. We would expect that biologically important human events such as attempts to communicate and establish affectional bonds would be patterned in time so as to be well matched to the infant's innate response biases. We now accept that the design of the human face is such that its visual stimulus characteristics closely match the evolved innate visual preferences of the human infant. I am here expanding this concept to include the temporal patterning of human social behaviors.

What this fairly regular tempo may mean for the infant is intriguing. One central tendency of the infant's mental life is the formation and testing of hypotheses. The creation of expectancies (temporal as well as others) and the evaluation of deviations or discrepancies from the expected form a crucial part of this central tendency. Accordingly, an ideal temporal stimulus cannot be absolutely regular and fixed. It it were, there would be no deviations to evaluate and nothing to continue to engage the infant's mental process. He would habituate rapidly. If, on the other hand, the deviations from the expected were either too large or irregular for him to encompass, then he would presumably be incapable of perceiving them as deviations. That is to say, they would be unrelated to the expected referent. Once again, his interest and cognitive engagement could not be maintained. Our current notion of the infant's cognitive processes thus requires that a temporal stimulus best suited to maintain interest and engagement would have to have a generally regular tempo (to allow for the formation of expectancy) but with a limited, or at least lawful, variability (to engage and maintain his evaluative processes). The tempos that mothers establish during these episodes of engagement are ideally suited to maintain attention and cognitive involvement.

Finally, during an engagement episode, there is generally only one major intention, such as to get or to maintain the infant's attention, or to enter into a game such as mother-chase, infant-dodge. The major intention of the episode is generally played out with only a selected portion of the partner's total repertoire of behaviors. In this sense, an episode of engagement is somewhat analogous to a paragraph in writing: it is like a topic unit.

A time-out episode.   A time-out episode consists of a relative behavioral silence, where there is both vocal silence and a relative cessation of ongoing movements.[1] These pauses in the ongoing flow are necessarily longer in duration than any of the pauses within the sequence of discrete behaviors that make up an engagement episode, and we find that they are almost always longer in duration than three seconds. Time-outs are also generally accompanied by an interruption in the visual attention paid to the infant. Generally, this simply involves the caregiver's looking away from the infant and focusing her attention elsewhere. Shifts in visual attention from the infant's face to other body parts may also constitute such an interruption. In either case there need not be a change in the level of maternal behavioral activity. But the direction or focus of her acts will be altered.

Most time-out episodes seem to involve a change in attentional focus and behavioral activity together. A common example is when the caregiver simply sits back in her chair for a moment, quietly, often looking elsewhere, and waiting before reengaging her attention and reinitiating a new sequence of behaviors.

The episode of engagement and the subsequent time-out episode appear to function as retuning units in the regulation of the interaction. During each episode of engagement both mother and infant are trying to stay within the boundaries of the optional ranges of excitement and affect. The engagement episodes come to an end when an upper or lower boundary has been exceeded or threatens to be. More often the infant signals this. During the subsequent time-out episode, the interpersonal situation can be reassessed (almost always out of awareness), that is, the interactive trend with regard to levels and direction of attention, excitement, and affect can be evaluated, and on the basis of this information new immediate goal-correcting strategies are formulated and then tried during the next episode of engagement, and so on. Each engagement episode thus offers the opportunity of "resetting" the interaction on a different course. It is important to note that the time-out intervals are also potentially important retuning or resetting moments. Very often the caregiver uses these relative cessations in the interaction to calm down the interaction.

The repetitive run. The repeating run is a series of repeating behaviors which occurs in the course of the entire sequence of behaviors that make up an episode of engagement. Most episodes will include many separate repetitive runs. One of the commonplace yet striking features of what a mother actually does during a natural play session with her infant is the repetitiveness of her behavior. This repetitiveness is apparent both in what she says to her infant and in what she does with her face, head, and body. Snow, among others, has commented on the use of repetition by mothers to facilitate language acquisition and comprehension in the young child who is learning to speak.[2] The phenomenon I wish to focus on, however, is somewhat different and more general. Maternal behavior manifests or utilizes repetition in all modalities: vocalization; movement; facial expression; tactile and kinesthetic stimulation. Furthermore, mothers use repetition at early points in the infant's development (it can be seen in the newborn nursery) where considerations such as trying to get the baby to learn a repeated element cannot be at issue. The "instructional" use of repetition may best be considered to be a special use of this more general phenomenon.

The extent of repetition on the part of mothers is impressive. We find that whether we measure verbal behaviors or nonverbal behaviors, as much as 30 percent of all vocal utterances or all facial displays or movements (say a head nod) are repeats of the immediately preceding behavior. The average repetitive run is slightly more than three units in length.

Why mothers repeat themselves so much is an interesting question. Besides attempting to catch the infant's attention, the simplest answer is probably that they run out of different things to say and do in a situation where in fact it matters very little, if at all, what they say so long as they keep the stimulation coming. This explanation may appear to make the phenomenon of repetition unimportant—which is not at all the case. What is very important is the sounds she makes, not the words she says. From this point of view the repetitive run assumes its importance as a structural and functional unit in the interaction.

The entire flow of maternal social behaviors can be likened to a symphony, in which the musical elements are her changing facial expressions, vocalizations, movements, and touches. By analogy, up to this point, we have been concerned only with the different notes and phrases she uses, their range of volume, quality, and duration, and also in the variety of instruments in her repertoire. We are only now becoming concerned with how these elements are structured in time to produce larger units. We have just considered how different tempos are constructed and may operate. The repetitive run provides the mother with the means to create themes and variations. Most repetitive runs do not repeat the unit exactly, and some variation is progressively introduced, such as "Hello . . . Hellooo . . . Helllooooo!"

The crucial feature of the run is that it consists of a stimulus presentation immediately followed by a re-presentation of the stimulus, unchanged or slightly altered. The general form can be conceptualized as statement and restatement of a theme with or without variations. Over one half of the runs, vocal and non-verbal, involve variations. This form of theme and variation, as created by caregivers with their own behaviors, can take several forms. The theme and the variation can change from run to run. It can be the sounds which vary slightly at each successive presentation, or the stress, or the pitch, or the intensity, or several of these at the same time. Or the caregiver can switch into a different format of theme and variation where time becomes the variation, for example, "Hi honey . . . Hi honey . . . . . . Hi honey . . . . Hi honey." This is like the inverse of music. Instead of the beat remaining the same while the lyrics or melody changes, this is similar to a song where the lyrics are the beat that maintains the regularity of structure, while the time interval is the element that changes. Many types of music use this inverted form of theme and variation.

In any event, the caregiver has a powerful tool in the repetitive run. It allows her to present and re-present in slightly varied form every and any aspect of human communicative and expressive behavior. Since every important social act is likely to be repeated over and over again, with each and all of its communicative properties varied, the infant can better accommodate more and more categories of different human behaviors and constantly enlarge the scope of those categories. So the caregiver, in trying to engage the infant and have fun, as well as overcome boredom, will create themes and variations of sound and movement which the infant, by virtue of the nature of his mental processes, will gradually retranspose into the classes of human social behavior that he must understand and engage in.

A SPLIT-SECOND WORLD

Mother and infant, like all humans, socially interact in a split-second world. Our social behaviors flash by and are perceived more rapidly than we generally imagine. The average maternal vocalization or facial display or movement lasts well under a second. So do the corresponding baby behaviors. In one careful frame-by-frame film analysis of a play interaction, the great majority of maternal and infant behaviors were in the range of .3 to 1.0 seconds in duration.[3]

The way interactive behaviors are structured in time greatly influences how we think the interaction works, and what models we devise to explain its operation. Sometimes interactive behaviors are nicely and neatly separated in time. For instance, a mother behavior occurs and is followed by a baby behavior which after a slight delay is followed by the next mother behavior, and so it goes on. In this temporal sequence it is easy to conceive of each behavior as a response to the preceding behavior and, at the same time, a stimulus for the subsequent behavior. A stimulus-response chain, with the conceptual clarity of a tennis match where the ball goes back and forth from one to the other court, is the most reasonable explanatory model of how the interaction works casually—and what its format is choreographically. This is a model with which we are all quite comfortable. However, events as we find them are not so orderly. Most of the time, at least during an episode of engagement, mother and infant behaviors overlap. Even then, there is often enough time (reaction time) between the onset of one member's behavior and the onset of the other's, so that we can call the second behavior a response to the first. The model remains intact. Frequently, though, there is not enough time between the onset of each partner's behavior to think in terms of a response (the time between onsets is less than known reaction times). Presenting even more problems, the two partners can begin to act at the precise same instant, and our model of a simple stimulus-response chain starts to run into serious trouble.

When the mother and infant are acting synchronously, and well under reaction time, then we are forced to think that they are following a shared program. A better analogy for this model is the waltz, where both partners know the steps and music by heart and can accordingly move precisely together, as against the tennis-match analogy of the stimulus-response chain. How can we reconcile these diverse views or explanations of the inner working of the interactive dance between people? For the sake of later clarity, it is worth complicating the picture with a closer

look at the temporal domain of several other examples of interpersonal exchanges.

Where in time, and what in substance, is the main social stimulus? The answer is not always simple. For instance, if you see
someone you know and haven't seen for a while approaching
you on the street, you have a fairly exact program or expectancy
based on your previous relationship and the time passed since
you last met, of how many feet away, on the approach, both of
you will say "hi," how long the "hi" ought to last, and how much
animation it ought to convey. If on the basis of your understanding of where the relationship is, you perform and expect a
"hi" of at least 0.5 seconds, but receive an 0.3 second "hi," you
will probably walk away wondering if anything is the matter
and quickly flip back through the events since your last meeting.
On the other hand, if the "hi" lasted 0.8 seconds instead of the
expected 0.5, you might have wondered "what was that about?"
or, given another context, "what do they want?"

The important point about such experiences, which many
jokes are built on, is that it is not the apparent stimulus event itself (the "hi") which is most relevant and responded to, but
rather the extent to which a well-known (anticipated) program is
deviated from. A temporal mismatch of a few hundred milliseconds between the spoken stimulus and the expected stimulus
becomes the effective stimulus event. Furthermore, the effective
stimulus event did not occur until *after* the 0.3 second "hi" was
over and only began to occur 0.5 seconds into the too long "hi."
Much of the subtle use or abuse of manners (shared conventional
programs) occurs in this split-second domain. In this case, we
can only understand a stimulus and a response in terms of their
relationship to a performed behavioral program.

Another example, from a different and somewhat unlikely
human exchange, a boxing match, well exemplifies the problems
and complexities in understanding well-coordinated interactions. At one point I was interested, for unrelated reasons, in
knowing how fast a human could execute a large arm movement. To do this I analyzed a film of Muhammad Ali boxing,
and counted how many film frames it took him to throw a left
jab (1/24 of a second). He is supposed to have one of the quick-
est jabs in the history of heavyweights. During the first ("fresh")
round of the Ali-Mildenberger world heavyweight title bout in

1966, 53 percent of all of Ali's left jabs were of shorter duration than the generally agreed upon fastest visual reaction time of 180 milliseconds (see Figure 7). For that matter, 36 percent of Mildenberger's jabs were faster than 180 milliseconds, and he was not known for his speed. The point of this apparent detour is that a punch in boxing can not be considered the stimulus to which the response is a dodge or block, even though that is what commonsense would have guessed. According to our knowledge of reaction time (the time from first seeing the stimulus to the *onset* of the response), at least 53 percent or more of Ali's jabs should have connected, when in fact very few did. One can argue that Mildenberger was responding to some stimulus, some cue, that preceded the actual jab. However, a fighter of Ali's caliber does not telegraph his punches in advance, and accordingly the attempt to look back in time to find *the* effective stimulus event would very probably fail. Once again we are forced to look be-

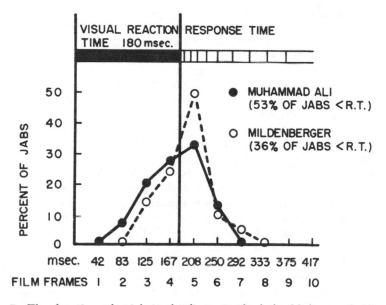

7. *The duration of a jab in the first round of the Muhammad Ali-Mildenberger world heavyweight title bout, 1966.*

yond *a* stimulus and *a* response, standing in isolation, and must view larger sequences of patterned behavior (programs). It is more reasonable to consider a punch or a dodge as a hypothesis-probing or generating attempt on each fighter's part to understand and predict the other man's behavioral sequences—or to force him into a more restricted repertoire of programs which is accordingly more predictable. Viewed this way, the successful punch reflects one fighter's ability to decode the other fighter's ongoing behavioral sequence, so that the other fighter's next move is correctly anticipated in time and space. What is truly amazing is how expert humans are at rapidly acquiring temporal and spacial "maps" of another person's behavioral sequences, even when a major point of an activity such as boxing is to keep the behavioral sequences in constant flux and as unpredictable as possible.

The boxing example is instructive in demonstrating how predictable our behavioral programs truly are even when they are designed not to be. In contrast then, when the goal of an activity is to display and share behavioral programs, the speed and accuracy with which we can form temporal-spatial schema of another's behavioral flow is not so surprising.

Let us return to the waltz again as an example of sharing a joint program. In the previous examples of the "hi" and the boxing match, we found that we needed to bring in the notion of programs. When we look closely at the waltz as an obvious example of a shared program, we will find that we must bring back some straightforward stimulus-response explanations. We can start at any point in the waltz. The leading partner must indicate to the following partner at the end of a measure which way they will turn or rotate. This signal is transmitted through hand pressure, body inclination, and such. Once that stimulus is responded to and the immediate course is set, the two partners can follow the known program and move in synchrony for a short period, "one, two three—one, two three," until a new decision point is reached at the end of a measure or two; a new stimulus-response interchange resets the general direction of movement the two will take when they reenter the jointly programmed portion of "one, two three." The more they have danced together, the longer sequences of programmed patterns they can string together without requiring a lead stimulus and a following response.

It appears that virtually all complex social human activities, including most interpersonal exchanges, require the simultaneous consideration of programmed behavioral sequences and of the stimulus-response paradigm. In every situation we encounter, both are operating. At moments the interaction is best conceptualized (and experienced?) as a stimulus-response dyadic process and at other moments as a programmed dyadic behavioral sequence. It switches back and forth.

There is an important assumption underlying the entire discussion up to this point. It is that adults (and probably infants) have the ability to estimate and reproduce quite accurately intervals of time and sequences of time intervals. Without considerable abilities in this realm the 200 millisecond difference between a spoken "hi" of 0.3 seconds and an expected "hi" of 0.5 seconds could never constitute a stimulus event; nor could a fighter ever land a successful punch unless he can accurately estimate where the target will be at exactly so many milliseconds in the future; nor could the waltz be jointly performed. As we shall see, the infant must be similarly equipped in some fashion to deal with the temporal world of his social interactions.

So we must explore what is known about human timing to help point the way to a further understanding of these events. We know from studies on the adult's abilities to estimate and anticipate intervals of time that we possess several different modes of timing. For very short intervals of time under 550 milliseconds, we have available a method called Absolute Timing with which we are extremely accurate in estimating or reproducing these short intervals.[4] One of the features of Absolute Timing is that within this range we have the same small variability or error in estimation regardless of the duration of the interval being timed. In other words, when estimating an interval of 250 milliseconds we could be off by say 15 milliseconds on either side, and when estimating an interval of 500 milliseconds we would be off by the same 15 milliseconds.

Most music is played in this range of maximally accurate timing covered by the Absolute Timing process. The interval between beats in range of music spanned by adagio, andante, allegro, and presto is from .63 to .29 seconds. Within this range very small deviations from regularity of beat are readily detectable, and we can extremely accurately anticipate the next beat.

When human beings have to estimate intervals of time larger

than about half a second, different modes of timing are utilized. The two best studied are Poisson Timing and Scalar Timing.[5] One of the important features of both of these modes of timing is that, unlike Absolute Timing, as the duration of the interval to be estimated gets larger, the accuracy of the estimate gets progressively less, but in different ways for each.

We have frightfully little direct evidence about the infant's timing capabilities. Yet it is difficult to understand how the infant could react as he does, as well as begin to comprehend his social universe, if he (or his nervous system if you prefer) were not capable of some fairly impressive time-estimating operations. After all, every event, including the complex social behaviors of caregivers and infants, unfolds in the dimension of time, and the timing itself of social behaviors often holds the key to the signal value or meaning or effect. Also, as has been pointed out, the kinds of interactions that are possible depend to a large extent on what abilities exist between the partners for anticipating (making a time estimation of) when the next behavior ought to occur. Sharing programs of behavioral sequences depends on this.

What do we know about the use of timing in caregiver-infant social interactions? Caregivers in playing with infants rely considerably on singing and other regular and rapid forms of sound stimulation, such as clapping, clucking, clicking, "tsking," most all of which have a tempo faster than one beat every half second. Furthermore, caregivers seem to use effectively the drift or progressive change in tempo, or sometimes a sudden but small change in tempo, to influence the infant's ongoing state of arousal or affect. This would suggest that within this range of intervals, of less than a half second, with repeated stimulation the infant becomes conditioned to the beat: he forms temporal expectancies of when the next beat will fall and is responsive to, at some level, small changes in tempo.

This happens in a variety of common situations. For instance, when an infant becomes overexcited and begins to emit the "ah ah ah" sound of the fuss-cry, the caregiver will often speed up her rate of behavior to "top" or override the baby's. She then slowly and progressively decreases the tempo of her speech or movement and in doing so acts like a pacemaker to quiet or soothe the baby. It sounds like: "Hey. Hey. Hey. Yeah . . Yeah

... Okay .... there ..... there we go ...... Yeah ....
that's better now ..... what was the matter, honey?" Similarly
the caregiver can use this general format in reverse, to help
arouse a baby and heighten his level of excitement.

The issue of infant timing is also quite relevant to the
important use of the repetitive run. The run permits the caregiver to present social stimuli in a form of theme with variations.
One of the major variations in subsequent repeats is often the
timing itself. One of the more dramatic illustrations of this
brings us back to an example used in a previous chapter: the "I'm
gonna get you" repeated game: "I'm gonna get you . . . I'mm
gooonna getcha ...... I'mmm gooooonnnaaa getcha." In this
sequence, the caregiver progressively "stretches" the interval of
the anticipated beat and in doing so increases the degree of discrepancy from the expected and the infant's excitement. There
could be no such effect, however, unless the infant had some
mechanism for timing the beat and forming a temporal estimate
of when the next beat should fall. The difference between the infant's estimate and mother's delayed performance is what constitutes the suspenseful and exciting discrepancy.

During an episode of engagement, caregivers generally establish a roughly regular tempo of behavioral production, be it in
the vocal or nonverbal mode or both. Furthermore, we saw how
some regularity was essential to permit the possibility or necess-
ity of forming expectancies (hypothesis generating) and also that
a certain amount of small but lawful variability around the average tempo was essential to engage and maintain the infant's evaluative processes. Accordingly, the infant is exposed to the somewhat variable tempo of a string of caregiver behaviors.

The timing problem for the infant is this. From episode to episode the caregiver may switch the tempo of her behaviors. She
may speed up or slow down. For instance, she may change from
producing a behavior (an utterance say) roughly every two
seconds to a slower rate of one every three seconds. When the
interval between behaviors gets larger than half a second, the
ability to estimate when the next behavior will fall becomes less
accurate. In other words, variability in estimation becomes
greater as the interval to be estimated becomes longer. When the
mother makes a change in tempo, the infant has to have some
way of figuring out what the new rate is and how much varia-

tion in the new tempo is acceptable or appropriate to the new tempo.

Recently we measured a number of different tempos that mothers use and the amount of variability associated with each tempo. As the interval between maternal behaviors got longer, the standard deviation about the tempo increased proportionally as the interval got longer.[6] The changing maternal tempos and their variability followed the model of a scalar timing process. Accordingly we postulated that the infant might well have a scalar unit timer for estimating social behaviors in the range beyond half a second. Such a timer "acts" like a rubber band with a dot in the middle so that, whether it is expanded or contracted, the dot is always in the middle. Similarly, the unit timer can be set, expanded, or contracted to a unit of time to be estimated, so that the appropriate variability around the unit to be timed also expands or contracts in proportion to the size of the unit. If the infant has a scalar unit timer, then the caregiver can switch to any tempo and the infant will readjust his unit timer to estimate the new average beat and the new range of variability appropriate to the new beat. In this fashion, his ability to form expectancies and to evaluate deviations from the expected will remain intact across the wide range of behavioral tempos a caregiver may use. Furthermore, unless the infant were equipped with this timing process, or a similar one, he could only react to—follow or lead—the caregiver but never dance *with* her.

The ability to estimate and anticipate intervals of time clearly relates to and even determines the various kinds of interactive processes that are possible. We know that mothers and infants can and do run off chained stimulus-response sequences. We also know that at times they jointly perform sequences that require anticipatory "knowledge" of the other's behavioral flow. Finally, we know that much of the social interactive process between them involves the subtle and smooth moving to and from one pattern of interaction to the other, so that the interactive stream continues uninterrupted. However, we still need to know much more about the nature and extent of the infant's timing abilities which allow him to participate in the intricate process of interpersonal exchange, and to form the internal mental representations that a relationship is built upon.

7 / From Interaction to Relationship

Up to this point we have been talking about infant-caregiver interactions. We must now begin to talk about the infant-caregiver relationship and how it emerges from the many interactions that contribute to its formation. This is a difficult leap. A relationship is certainly determined by the history of all the separate interactions, but implies more than the sum of past and present interactions. Conceptually it is a different kind of organization, or a different integration of experience. One of its central features is an enduring mental image, or schema, or representation of the other person. In most psychological theories, beginning with psychoanalysis, this enduring internal representation is the sine qua non of object permanence.

When can we speak of an infant as being in a relationship? There is no hard and fast answer. However, by the latter part of the first year of life the infant shows a number of behaviors that strongly suggest that we can begin to talk about relationships. Sometime around the ninth month of life the infant manifests what is called the stranger reaction. This reaction can vary widely from mild wariness to extreme distress at the approach of or in the presence of a stranger.[1] Shortly after the stranger reaction appears, most infants begin to manifest a "separation reaction" when the primary caregiver leaves their presence and a "reunion reaction" when she returns. The separation reaction is one of distress, but here too the intensity varies greatly from infant to infant. The reunion reaction is one of joy and involves the performance of affiliative behaviors.

It is generally assumed that these developmental landmarks taken together indicate that the infant has formed a specific attachment to a single person, his primary caregiver. They indicate as well that the infant is beginning to consolidate an internal representation of her, so that some degree of object permanence is in evidence. At this point one can finally talk about an actual relationship with someone who is to a large extent, at least, separated from the self. There is still some controversy about the nature of these landmarks as well as how much can be inferred from them. Nonetheless, it is a fair guess that toward the end of the first year of life the infant has made a significant leap toward the establishment of relationships. We really do not know whether there is a true "leap" in development or whether a gradual process becomes suddenly more visible because of other related developmental changes. We do know that the process is by no means finished at this point. In any event, enough has happened by the latter part of the first year that we must ask how prior events have contributed to this developmental advance.

The task in front of us now is thus to try to conceptualize how an enduring internal representation, as the cornerstone of a relationship, could emerge from the interactive experiences we have been considering so far. We do not in fact know how this feat is accomplished. We will have to speculate and extrapolate from what we do know about how internal mental schemas of inanimate objects are formed, and from the thoughtful reconstructions of psychoanalysts who have grappled with the problem of the early representations of primary caregivers. Hereafter, I will follow the convention of using the term "schemas" when referring to the internalization of inanimate objects and the term "representations" when referring to those of people. Why not use the same terms and conceptualize the same process for both inanimate and animate objects? The main reason is intuitive. The nature and subjective feel of our relationship with things seems qualitatively different from that with human beings. Through associative links one can act and feel toward an object as one would toward the person it is associated with. This is a very common experience. The reverse experience is quite rare. There is also no question that one can have a "pure" (unassociated to any particular other human) emotional response to an object such as a tree or beautiful stone. However, I wonder to what extent these experiences were, in the course of evolution, initially "designed in" for the purpose of responding to humans, but by virtue of man's extraordinary plasticity were transferred so that, in the right setting, they can also be released by inanimate objects.

Infants certainly show obvious emotions, such as delight, in their interactions with rattles and other toys. But the question in this situation is whether their emotional response is related to the object per se or to the experience with their own processes of mastery or recognition. I would guess the latter, and assume that the affective experience is between the infant as actor and the infant as self-observer and evaluator.

Some evidence that bears on this distinction suggests, but does not conclude, that the infant's experience with objects and people is of a significantly different nature. Berry Brazelton and his colleagues have reported that the quality of an infant's bodily movement in the presence of objects is different, more jerky and less flowing, from that seen in the presence of people.[2] Sylvia Bell finds that the timetable for the establishment of object schema and people representations may proceed along different developmental courses.[3]

THE FORMATION OF SCHEMAS

Piaget's work on the formation of schemas of inanimate objects during the first years of life remains the most comprehensive and influential. Piaget postulated that, during the first years, the formation of mental schemas proceeds by way of the internalization of actions and the sensations and perception that result from these actions. An action schema thus consists of two fused elements: the act the infant makes toward or upon an object and the sensory experience provided by the object, which is largely determined by the particular action the infant performed. Let us take one particular rattle in an infant's crib as an example. Initially, action schemas for the following separate sensorimotor events get established: gazing at the rattle and what those movements feel like; holding the rattle and what it feels like; shaking it and what that sounds like.

There are thus two distinct "elements" of the experience. There is the action that is a muscular and proprioceptive *motor experience*, and there is the *sensory experience* emanating from the object—the particular stimulus properties of the object which are perceivable in the course of the particular action performed. The motor experience and the sensory experience are always intimately connected and are experienced as a single unit of experience. Each of these sensori-motor units must be practiced and experienced over and over before the specific unit of experience is internalized to become a specific schema in the mind.

At the same time that each of these sensori-motor schemas is being consolidated internally, there occurs a growing intercoordination among them. Internal linkages become established between the separate schemas to produce a network that emerges as a larger or higher-order schema of the rattle, since it consists of an integration of all of the separate sensori-motor schemas: the rattle as viewed, reached for, grasped, held, shaken, heard.

Now suppose that a second and different kind of rattle is given to the baby in his crib. On first exposure, the infant has no way to know that this new object is also a rattle. He will utilize the same operations he learned from his interaction with the first rattle and by so doing reorganize and expand his schema of the first rattle so that it can also encompass the second rattle. In this way he creates a larger schema of different objects that can be viewed and seen; reached for and motion-experienced; held and felt; shaken and heard. The result is a schema of a *class* of objects: rattles, which can be viewed, seen, reached for, grasped, felt, shaken, and heard. It is in this fashion that mental schemas grow.

It is important to note that what is initially internalized as a schema is not the object itself or alone, nor the action itself, but rather an interaction between the infant and the object, that is, an active "object relation" in the form of a sensori-motor schema.

THE FORMATION OF REPRESENTATIONS OF PEOPLE

In considering the internalization of sensori-motor units of experience into mental schemas of objects such as rattles, we had only two elements to deal with: the motor experience of the act and the sensory experience from the object. In an interaction with an alive, active human participant, in which the joint behaviors of the infant and the "object" (caregiver) result in internal changes in the infant's excitation and affect, we have a third element to deal with: the infant's excitatory-affective experience. For the sake of brevity, I shall call this element the infant's "affective experience," cautioning that it importantly includes the infant's state of excitation or activation as well as affect, and that at times it is only the former that is manifest and the latter is inferred.

INTERPERSONAL PROCESS UNITS

Consider for a minute the fact and problem discussed in the previous chapter, that all events unfold in time. Human behavior is almost always changing, and even internal experiences of excitation and affect undergo momentary changes in intensity and direction. The smile of a caregiver provides a case in point. Does the infant perceive and experience the smile as a still shot, like a photograph, or as a movement sequence of short duration patterned in time and space, like a motion-picture clip? We know that sounds and perhaps internal feelings are experienced only over time—that is, an instantaneous "slice" of sound or affect has no coherent meaning or recognizable form. We suspect that the same is true for perceptions of the smile and other visualized human behaviors.

I am suggesting that, at least in the realm of human interactive behaviors, there is a basic process unit of interactive experience. This process unit is not necessarily the smallest unit of perception in any modality, but rather is the smallest unit in which a temporally dynamic interactive event with a beginning, middle, and end can occur. Such a process unit is like the briefest incident or vignette that can contain a sensory, motor, and affective element of experience and, accordingly, have signal value as an interpersonal event.

A vocal utterance, or the formation-maintenance-decomposition of a facial expression, could define the boundaries of an interpersonal process unit. So too would discrete head movements, most kinesthetic (a bounce) and tactile (a touch or tickle) stimulus events, and most infant acts. All of these events occur in roughly the same temporal domain of from about a third of a second to a little under a few seconds in duration. These interpersonal process units may be the units of sensori-motor-affective experience that are initially internalized as the separate representation of another person.

There are some suggestive bits of clinical evidence that indicate the existence of such units. If you ask someone to "think of your mother or of your father," they will generally report the memory of a dynamic moment or two that corresponds fairly closely to what I am calling interpersonal process units. In many other such situations of thinking about another person, the "pieces" that tumble out of memory are roughly of this size and composition. This is not to make a definite claim that such experiential units exist as described and are the building blocks of internal representations. On the contrary, I am saying that we have a conceptual need for a functional unit like this and what I have sketched is no more than a tentative working description of such a unit.

THE SENSORY EXPERIENCE

The sensory experience is the infant's perception of the stimulus events provided by the caregiver. As we have seen, the caregiver provides a vast array of sights, sounds, and tactile and kinesthetic sensations. The central question is: How does the infant form the sensory "element" of the representation from these events? Let us begin with the sights and, for the sake of an example, focus on the caregiver's facial expressions. From the infant's viewpoint, in the beginning there is no reason to assume that the mother's face displaying a smile is considered the same face, or even the same object, as when she is displaying a frown. It is similar to the problem of the two different rattles.

It seems reasonable, even obvious, that the manner in which caregivers perform infant-elicited facial expressions greatly contributes to the infant's ability to form sensory representations of these expressions. The first way this is done is through exaggeration in performance, especially of those features most characteristic of the particular facial expression. This behavioral underlining of the crucial elements must facilitate the infant's recognitory processes. Second, generally each facial expression is bounded by a relative behavioral silence, at least more so than is seen in adult-adult interactions. By doing this, the mother puts each expression in a discrete package, separated out from the ongoing flow. Accordingly, each unit of behavior is more recognizable and the problem of slowly discriminating where one thing begins and another ends, and thereby isolating each separate unit, is somewhat circumvented. Third, we do not know the rate at which infants process information. Presumably it is slower than adult rates and speeds up with age. If the caregiver did not slow down many of her behaviors as one of the features of infant-elicited variations, her behavior might flash by too quickly for the infant's immature rate of processing perceptual information, especially visual sequences. The mother might then look like a figure in an early silent film, moving so jerkily and with such lapses in movement continuity that the infant would be unable to hold in mind the constancy of the object across its many disjointed transformations. The infant could never capture and hold a movement sequence and never be able to perceive and assimilate unitary behavioral events, such as smiles or any facial expression or patterned bodily movement.

Last, because of the great amount of repetitiveness in maternal behaviors the infant is constantly exposed to repeating runs, in which an expression can be presented in the form of a theme with variations. Each successive smile, for example, will be slightly different from the last but still belongs to the same class of events: smiles. In this way, the repetitive run may greatly enhance the infant's acquisition of the classes of behaviors a caregiver performs. By the end of the sixth month the infant is capable of differentiating different facial expressions as displayed in pictures.[4] We would assume that his discriminative ability in terms of the expressive repertoire of his mother's actual face would be even greater.

In this fashion the infant can gradually form the sensory elements of representations of different expressions, different vocalizations, different movements. As each is being consolidated, intercoordinations among them become established into a higher-order sensory representation of the caregiver as a source of various stimulations which are integrated classes of behaviors in different modalities. A clear example of this kind of intercoordination of sensory representations across different modalities occurs in the experiment referred to earlier: the expectation by infants at three months that the visual image of the mother's face and the sound of her voice should emanate from the same place.

THE MOTOR EXPERIENCE

The second internalized "element" of the sensori-motor-affective unit of experience consists of the infant's actions, the proprioceptive experience of the act that is his own behavior. These actions include the infant's gazing behavior (whether he looks at all, whether he gazes directly from a full-face positon or sideways from an averted position, or whether he views with peripheral vision); his head movements; facial displays; vocalizations; and body movements. We can speculate that the infant experiences and encodes these behaviors as interpersonal process units just as the sensory experience of the caregiver's behavior is experienced by him in the same process units.

One of the most crucial points about the infant's motor experience is that it largely determines the nature of his sensory experience. This is true in several senses. He can change his sensory experience of the caregiver by doing something that alters the caregiver's behavior. For instance, if he averts his head and eyes so that her behavior is viewed peripherally instead of seen from the face-to-face position, he will have an entirely different sensori-motor experience, even though the caregiver's behavior is objectively the same (from any point of view other than his). Or his motor experience can change his sensory experience by altering the caregiver's behavior. If he smiles and thereby elicits a smile in return, he will have accomplished this.

The simple situation just described raises a new issue. If he smiles and as he does so—experiencing the sensations from his own facial muscles—sees that her face does *not* change for a palpable interval of time, and then bursts into a smile, he has a very particular sensori-motor experience—one that is highly conducive to learning the temporal format of contingency relationships (stimulus, pause for reaction time, response). If in another situation, he and his caregiver were for the moment locked into a brief shared program, then she might have begun to smile at the same time he did. An entirely different sensori-motor experience would have been created. A third possibility is that he smiles and her face does not change at all. The sensori-motor experiences associated with each situation may be needed for contrast so that the infant can begin to comprehend the concept of contingency in the sense that one behavior causes another.

We generally think of the infant during the first year as being entirely egocentric in the sense that he draws no boundary line between himself and another, or between his actions and those of another, and also that he imagines that his behavior causes or creates the behavior of others. How he learns to separate self from other is an open question, but the nature of his sensori-motor experience clearly offers him many opportunities to begin to pry apart the self-other fusion that is reflected in the sensori-motor fusion of his experience. Since the same motor experience can be accompanied by a variety of sensory experiences, only some of which are a predictable function of his motor behavior, the self-other distinction must have one origin in the fact that any one motor experience can be coupled with a multiplicity of sensory experiences, some of which are more predictable than others.

On the one hand, I am pointing out the enormous extent to which the infant's sensory experience is determined by the nature of his motor experience, resulting in a fused experience. On the other hand, I am saying that to the extent that his sensory experience is not reliably determined by the nature of his motor experience, resulting in a multiplicity of sensori-motor experiences built around the same motor experience, to that extent he can begin to uncouple the self-other fusion.

A simple example of this uncoupling process can be seen in the often cited example of the infant's "magical control" of making things or people disappear and reappear simply by closing and reopening his eyes or by fully averting his gaze and then returning it. What is usually omitted in this example is that when he looks again the image and position of the person may or may not have been transformed. The fused sensori-motor experience is a double-edged sword. It creates an internal union with another in the form of an internal representation and, at the same time, contributes to the disunion of the self from the other in the external world.

THE AFFECTIVE EXPERIENCE

The infant and the caregiver jointly contribute to the regulation of the infant's state of attention, excitation, and affect. We have seen how the caregiver uses her behaviors as stimuli to alter the infant's internal state. We have also seen how the infant regulates his own internal state. In a real sense, the momentary changes in the infant's excitation and affect are both a product and a cause of the interaction between the caregiver's goal-corrected stimulations and the infant's goal-corrected regulating actions. From the infant's viewpoint these powerful internal changes and sensations are probably not experienced as belonging exclusively to the caregiver's stimulation (the sensory experience), nor are they experienced as belonging exclusively to his own actions (the motor experience). It is more likely that they are experienced as part of an undifferentiated compound experience including what the caregiver does, what the infant does, and what that feels like internally.

In order to examine these internal units of experience more closely, we shall artificially isolate them for the moment. These experiences, stripped of sensori-motor context, include feelings such as having one's attention captured and a feeling of increasing excitement and pleasurable expectancy; experiencing a gradual rise in pleasurable or unpleasurable excitation; experiencing a rapid rise in excitation accompanied by wariness or unpleasure or delight; experiencing a decrease in excitation accompanied by an increase in well-being or by a loss in pleasure and the onset of something akin to boredom; experiencing the reversal of a downtrend in excitation and the feeling of pleasure on the upswing; experiencing unpleasure with overexcitation; experiencing the maintenance of a level of pleasure with a shift in excitation. The various combinations of different levels or changes in excitation and affect are many, but correspond to common and recognizable moments of internal experience. It is important to note that we are mainly concerned with shifts in level and changes in direction of affect and excitation, that is, with the nodal points of fluctuations in internal feelings. This emphasis on the change points is dictated by two concerns: first, these moments are the most likely to have high stimulus value (by virtue of contrast); and second, the temporal duration and nature of such nodal moments most likely correspond to what I have called interpersonal process units.

REPRESENTATIONS AS INTERNALIZED UNITS OF EXPERIENCE

A sensori-motor-affective unit of experience is hard to describe simply. Such an experience, for example, could be what it feels like to smile, see the caregiver smile, and experience an internal pleasurable feeling of mounting excitement. This is one fused unit of interpersonal experience. Another such might be what it feels like to perceive a looming face, and experience a rapid rise in excitation that is negatively toned, and perform a sharp head aversion that attenuates the intensity of the perception and the internal feeling.

A social interaction between infant and caregiver consists, for the infant, of hundreds of such experiential units strung together. Furthermore, these sensori-motor-affective units occur over and over during each social interaction in every day. The infant thus has ample opportunity to internalize each unit as a separate representation.

We do not know how these units get internalized, except that quite clearly memory traces of them must be formed and stored. We have speculated that the "size" of the experiential units that are internalized corresponds to an interpersonal process unit, and consists of a coherent moment of interactive experience. Further, for a unit of experience to get internalized as a representation it must contain all three elements. The situation can be likened to a key opening a lock. The key is the sensori-motor-affective unit of experience. The lock that opens the door permitting an experience to be encoded internally as a representation is made of three tumblers, and each of the tumblers, a sensory, motor, and affective tumbler, must all be turned into place for the lock to open. One of the important implications of this formulation is that there can be no representations without an affective component. Schema, on the other hand, can be formed from sensori-motor experiences alone.

After each separate sensori-motor-affective unit of experience is internalized as a single representation, what is the fate of these initially isolated representations? How do they cluster, organize, and integrate to form larger more ordered representations? Through processes, perhaps not so different from those assumed for the interaction of schemas, representations become interconnected. Linkages between related representations form networks of representations. The networks integrate to establish a progressively more comprehensive representation to the other person—or more accurately of the interpersonal experience of being with the other person. In this sense, once the representation has become sufficiently inclusive it is tantamount to a relationship that exists, or is carried on, within the mind.

Once the infant has formed even a moderately comprehensive representation, he can be said to bring to each new interactive event a history of the relationship, in the form of the representation. This "history" then affects the course of each new interaction. Similarly, the sensori-motor-affective experience of each new interaction, once internalized, may alter the configuration of the history as it progresses. A dynamic interaction thus evolves between the past and the present, between established representations and current exchanges, between the relationship and the ongoing interaction. Conceived in this fashion, it is quite understandable that each infant-caregiver pair can develop an individual course for their own relationship, and that the outcome of seemingly similar interactions can be quite divergent for different pairs with different histories. Relationships thus take on directon and momentum.

It also seems necessary to postulate here that the mind has something like a cross-referencing system so that all of the sensory images of a person, for example—or all of the encoded affects of a certain kind—can be partially uncoupled from the other component elements of the representation and be "resorted" or reintegrated to form strictly sensory part-representations or affective part-representations. The relative ability and ease with which the three elements of a representation can be reversibly uncoupled, integrated, disassembled, and recoupled brings us to some fascinating questions that have long occupied psychiatry and psychoanalysis. It is a common clinical phenomenon to find the affective component of an experience or representation split off from the sensori-motor component, so that only the latter is available to awareness. For instance, the memory of an emotional scene with a loved one can be recalled in exquisite visual and verbal detail, but the feelings associated with the incident remain out of awareness. The reverse is also found, where strong feelings are experienced or recalled but are unattached and disintegrated from their sensori-motor context. We have no way of knowing to what extent similar disjunctions can occur in infancy during the early period of representation formation. However, the concepts of forming and ultimately uniting representations of the "good" and "bad" mother, as formulated by Margaret

Mahler and others,[5] require some fluidity in disassembling and reassembling in different configurations the component parts from different representations.

Because this examination of the activities between infants and caregivers has centered almost exclusively on the playful social interactions during a short span of development, we can only draw a partial picture of the relationship. To arrive at a fuller picture, what I have described for the play period must also be described for feeding, diapering, bathing, and so on. Since each of these activities involves some quite different and even unique sensori-motor-affective experiences, it is conceivable, even likely, that the infant integrates different representations of the caregiver as she is experienced in the separate activities, say a "feeding mother" who is different from the "playing mother." In the beginning these separate integrations may overlap only slightly and very gradually merge to form a unified representation of the caregiver across all activities. However, playful interactions, as we have seen, have a way of emerging spontaneously in the course of almost any and all activities. In this way, the constant reappearance of the "playing mother" in the course of an experience with the "feeding mother" and with the "bathing mother" may help to facilitate the infant's integration of a fully consolidated representation.

The entire process of forming a relationship never stops, even in adulthood. It is even more dramatic for the infant, who is so rapidly changing that, by force of growth and development alone, he will constantly bring new motor experiences and sensory and affective capabilities to his interactions. His relationships and representations are always expanding, changing, reforming.

8 / Missteps in the Dance

The infant is a virtuoso performer in his attempts to regulate both the level of stimulation from the caregiver and the internal level of stimulation in himself. The mother is also a virtuoso in her moment-by-moment regulation of the interaction. Together they evolve some exquisitely intricate dyadic patterns. It takes two to create these patterns, which sometimes look ominous for the future course of development and sometimes look quite effortlessly beautiful.

We accept that the nature of our earliest relationships greatly influences the course of relationships to come. After all, in this early period the infant is learning what to expect from, how to deal with, and how to be with a particular human being. For quite some time the infant has limited opportunities to learn that there is any way to "be with" another person other than the particular way he is coming to know.*

If we could capture the essence of the nature of characteristic interactive patterns of any individual infant-caregiver pair, it might be possible, even feasible, to predict and chart the likely course of future interpersonal relatedness. Yet this task eludes us. Both parents and researchers maintain that some tempera-

*There is a small but rapidly growing interest and literature on the father as primary caregiver. Even more relevant, however (statistically speaking at least), are questions about the effect of the secondary caregiver on expanding, rerouting, or disrupting the patterns created by the powerful impact of the primary caregiver. This is clearly an area of vitally needed knowledge. It relates not only to most fathers but to all extended family and other "secondary" caregivers. The very issue of potency of effect of primary versus secondary caregivers may prove to be a misleading dichotomy. Both may be crucial in different and most likely complementary ways.

mental features of infants, such as activity level, remain consistent during development.[1] Furthermore, at a different level, most parents experience that the interpersonal "feel" of what it is like to be with the person who is their child maintains some indescribable yet pervasively recognizable unbroken strain from infancy on, even though the manifestation of this "feel" may change considerably during different developmental epochs. We have all experienced this in most of our long-term relationships.

Nonetheless, it is difficult to predict the future outcome of any given mother-infant interaction. When actually watching the emergence of these early relationships, unless the infant is obviously and grossly deviant or damaged, or the mother grossly neglecting or physically abusive, it is hard to tell whether one is watching the beginnings of a permanently maladaptive pattern, or a normal period of "messing up," or just the formation of an individualized, even idiosyncratic but natural fit between a particular infant and a particular caregiver. A case illustration will serve here.

One of the first mother-infant pairs I followed carried me along a difficult path which challenged and forced many reevaluations of my role as researcher-clinician. The journey I traveled with them engendered much restraint about predicting outcomes and evaluating the need and timing of interventions—a restraint that remains still.

I first met Jenny when she was almost three months old. Her mother was an animated woman who would clearly be categorized as intrusive, controlling, and overstimulating by most standards. She seemed to want, need, and expect a high level of exciting, animated interaction, always keeping the level of stimulation hovering about the upper boundary of Jenny's optimal range of tolerance. Furthermore, the mother seemed to want the level she wanted when she wanted it.

The dance they had worked out by the time I met them went something like this. Whenever a moment of mutual gaze occurred, the mother went immediately into high-gear stimulating behaviors, producing a profusion of fully displayed, high-intensity, facial and vocal infant-elicited social behavior. Jenny invariably broke gaze rapidly. Her mother never interpreted this temporary face and gaze aversion as a cue to lower her level of behavior, nor would she let Jenny self-control the level by gaining distance. Instead, she would swing her head around following Jenny's to reestablish the full-face position. Once the mother achieved this, she would reinitiate the same level of stimulation with a new arrangement of facial and vocal combinations. Jenny again turned away, pushing her face further into the pillow to try to break all visual contact. Again, instead of holding back, the mother continued to chase Jenny. The pillow and side wing of the infant seat now prevented the mother from swinging around to the face-to-face position. So this time, she moved closer, in an apparent attempt to break through and establish contact. She also escalated the level of her stimulation even more by adding touching and tickling to the unabated flow of vocal and facial behaviors. (Anecdotally, most observers viewing this kind of intrusiveness experience it as almost physically painful to sit still and watch. It engenders feelings of impotent rage and is often accompanied by a tightening in the gut or a headache.)

With Jenny's head now pinned in the corner, the baby's next recourse was to perform a "pass-through." She rapidly swung her face from one side to the other right past her mother's face. When her face crossed the mother's face, in the face-to-face zone, Jenny closed her eyes to avoid any mutual visual contact and only reopened them after the head aversion was established on the other side. All of these behaviors on Jenny's part were performed with a sober face or at times a grimace.

The mother followed her to the new side, producing volleys of stimulation that again progressively pushed Jenny's head farther away until she performed another pass-through. After a series of these "failures," the mother would pick the infant up from the infant seat and hold her under the armpits, dangling in the face-to-face position. This maneuver usually succeeded in reorienting Jenny toward her, but as soon as she put Jenny back down, the same pattern reestablished itself. After several more repeats of these sequences the mother became visibly frustrated, angry, and confused and Jenny, quite upset. At that point the interaction was terminated and Jenny was put to bed.

The blatant nature of this kind of intrusive behavior makes it difficult not to infer some unconscious maternal hostility toward the infant or the caregiving role. From an observer's viewpoint it seems inconceivable that the mother can keep herself unaware of the aversive nature of the interaction. Yet it is quite possible from the standpoint of the participating caregiver not to see it. Also it is not always the case that such behavior has hostility as a major motivation. Enthusiastic well-motivated inexperience, coupled with interpersonal insensitivity, would produce similar actions.

In any event, the general pattern of mother-chase and infant-dodge is not at all an uncommon sequence. What was uncommon with Jenny and her mother was the unrelenting chase and the negative affect on both sides. We have seen the chase and dodge pattern between other mother-infant pairs operate as a delicately and mutually regulated game which does in fact keep the infant hovering about the upper limits of his tolerance for stimulation and excitement, but allows for the small adjustments that make it pleasurably exciting rather than aversive. In those situations, after the infant averts gaze (often with a slight smile), the mother waits a moment before chasing—a moment when the infant can self-regulate his internal state and begin to build up an anticipation of the mother's next move. Then when she finally does chase, she reinitiates the encounter at a lower level of stimulation, carefully building to higher and higher levels until the infant dodges away again.

At other times, the chase-dodge pattern is not so sequential in the stimulus-response sense, but has more of a shared synchronous programmatic sequence. In this case, after the infant dodges away, the mother predictably hesitates before going after him. She carefully measures out the interval of hesitation (and probably preparatory behaviors), so that at the same moment she moves to chase he can begin his dodge. Each pulls to a simultaneous stop again, still not facing each other but, importantly, without ever changing the amount of distance or contact between them, only toying with it.

The pattern between Jenny and her mother had none of that playfulness or lightness. After several weeks of visits, the basic pattern between them had not changed except that each seemed to have given up on the other a little. Jenny avoided eye contact with her mother more and more often, and the mother, while she did not alter her style, interacted less and spent more time just sitting. I became progressively more concerned when a week or so later Jenny's avoidance of eye contact was almost complete, her face aversions more pronounced and continuous, and her face almost expressionless.

As this situation worsened, I became positively alarmed. A large part of my alarm stemmed from the knowledge that the avoidance of eye contact and the face-to-face position is considered the most persistent and consistent feature of childhood autism.[2] Furthermore, it has been anecdotally reported that in some cases of later autism or childhood schizophrenia, this kind of visually turning off and away from the human environment can retrospectively be traced to the first half year of life. I was afraid I was watching the early onset of autism. The reason (perhaps luckily) that I had not acted before had to do with the particular way I "saw" the interaction, as dictated by my role as an experimenter. By that I do not mean any compunctions about disrupting an "experiment" with a needed intervention. The problem was both more simple and more complex. When I visited the home with the camera I watched only with a technical eye, attending to the angles, framing, lighting, and saw little else. Only after studying the TV tapes back in the laboratory during the following week or so did the behavioral and clinical story unfold for me. Only then did I "see" the interaction as a clinical entity. Accordingly, I was always a few weeks behind the breaking story. When I realized the potential seriousness of what was happening (what had actually happened two weeks ago) I consulted several co-workers for advice and immediately made another home visit. Jenny was now almost four months old. I brought the camera, but watched the interaction as a clinician, ready with the decision to intervene unless things had changed considerably. They had.

Somehow Jenny and her mother were achieving and maintaining more mutual gaze. The chase and dodge game, while still ominous-looking, had lightened enough so that it had some joyful teasing moments and a few smiles were seen. I said nothing that day, but instead went back to the laboratory to catch up on the weeks that I was behind, only to find that the improving trend had clearly started two weeks ago and I was simply watching its continuation. The story ends happily. The interaction continued to improve, though I have never been quite sure why. The mother lowered her level of stimulation only slightly and became only a bit less controlling and intrusive. Perhaps the greatest change occurred in Jenny, simply by virtue of maturation. (Two weeks, at three months of age, is a long time. As Burton White has shown, infants become increasingly able to tolerate larger doses of stimulation.[3]) Jenny seemed better able to handle the level and "dosing" of stimulation from her mother and in doing so began to give her mother more of the positive feedback that allowed the mother to alter her behavior. A vicious cycle was broken. The story of course does not end there. At each new phase of development Jenny and her mother have had to replay this basic scenario of overshoot and resolution, but with different sets of behaviors and at higher levels of organization. We do not yet know what strengths and assets or what weaknesses and deficits for the future course of her relatedness Jenny will ultimately emerge with.

I still wonder whether, if Jenny had been born with a greater sensitivity to stimulation or a more slowly maturing ability to regulate and thus tolerate progressively greater amounts of stimulation, would matters have turned out as well, and, if not, would a timely intervention have mattered? The opposite question also still remains open. Suppose I had intervened on the day of that visit, even though things were self-correcting. Would that have ultimately been better or worse? After all, they had begun to work it out on their own without the potential turbulence that an intervention can introduce.

The notion of the infant and caregiver mutually regulating and correcting or not correcting the moment-by-moment course of their interactions permits a perspective on two related clinical aspects of the relationship. First, what would be considered misregulations within the dyad or failures to goal-correct the levels of attention, excitement, and affect so that the optimal range is seldom maintained? Second, any goal-correcting act the infant makes can be considered a coping maneuver to adapt to or adjust the internal and external stimulation presented by the ongoing situation. The line between an early coping mechanism and an early defensive operation is thin. We thus find ourselves in a position to consider some of the origins of early coping mechanisms and defenses. It is crucial to remember that the infant's constant attempts at adaptation are synonymous, in this social situation, with his experience of what it is like to be with someone.

REGULATORY FAILURES AND OVERSTIMULATION

There are many routes to overstimulation and many different solutions or attempts at adaptive solutions. We can pass over the "causes" of overstimulation rapidly. The initial impetus may come from the caregiver or the infant. In either case, there is a mismatch. For our purposes the issue of primary responsibility is minor, when present at all, since the "organism" of interest, the "patient," is the dyad. Nonetheless it is necessary to describe, when possible, where the initial impetus of a potential misregulation comes from, even though our central interest is the way in which the dyad adjusts to the misregulation.

Controlling and intrusive behaviors by the caregiver are among the most common causes of overstimulation. When viewed blow by blow or instant by instant, most controlling behaviors involve interfering with the infant's self-regulatory behaviors. For instance, if an infant's gaze aversion is not respected and allowed to achieve its goal (as in the case of Jenny), the infant is deprived or robbed of one of his main self-regulating mechanisms for adapting to the level of stimulation. He may then be forced to develop more extreme regulating or terminating behaviors. Another simple example of such behavior may be seen in the course of a lively social interaction. If the infant shows a shift in direction of affect from positive to negative by suddenly changing from a smile to a sober face or grimace, the mother can once again respect and even reinforce this signal as a communication to ease off. Instead, the intrusive or controlling response would be for the caregiver to escalate dramatically the intensity, complexity, and richness of her behavioral display. If she does that, she will usually succeed for an instant in refocusing the infant's attention on her. But in the immediately following instant the infant will show even greater signs of distress or unhappiness. The important point is that during that momentary sequence the infant will have lost an opportunity to learn that he can successfully regulate the external world, and as a by-product his inner state, through the use of an emotional communication. Losing one opportunity means little. However, if such experiences are chronic, the infant may learn either that his facial displays of emotion are not relevant communicative events to change the world or, worse, that they are but will make matters worse. The issue at stake is momentous. The infant requires the integrative experience of having his motor experiences, which are associated with affective states, successfully restructure the external world, successfully in the sense of changing the affective state in the desired or needed direction. If they do not, the motor expression of affectivity will more likely be progressively inhibited and the infant will gradually cease to perform affective facial expressions.

There are two other points hidden in these examples of controlling and intrusive behavior. The first is that, to be controlling, it is necessary to be extremely sensitive to interactive changes and cues. You have to be just as reactive to interpersonal cues in order to misrespond as you do to respond "correctly." Paradoxically, then, controlling and intrusive behaviors on the part of the caregiver may require a considerable degree of responsivity. This leads to the second point. Suppose the infant is constitutionally somewhat lethargic or hypoactive or has a degree of developmental lag. In these situations, caregiving behaviors that would look "appropriate" for a normal infant might look controlling or intrusive. The caregiver, in fact, may be well aware that her behavior in this match or context is controlling or intrusive, but she may have opted (consciously or unconsciously) to stretch her infant's responsiveness to stimulation and engender more animation in him, even at the temporary expense of tampering with his developing self-regulatory mechanisms. In the long run she may well prove right.

The issue of match between the caregiver's behavior, the expectation of what *her* infant's behavior ought to be like, and what that infant's behavior really is can never be overlooked, as Escalona has fully shown us. Sometimes both caregiver and infant clearly fall within a normal range of stimulus tolerance and stimulation, but at opposite ends of the spectrum. Again, a mismatch could potentially result in a controlling and intrusive dyadic situation or a different resolution could get worked out.

In contrast to controllng behaviors, insensitivity to the infant's behavior on the part of an animated or overenthusiastic caregiver will also result in a failure of regulation. In this situation, however, the caregiver simply misses the infant's interpersonal cues and self-regulatory attempts to lower the ambient level of stimulation. Accordingly, she makes no goal-correcting changes.

What the infant does matters relatively little. His behavior (within limits) will not make things either better or worse. I have the impression that the "lock-in" or quality and tightness of bonding in such pairs is less than that seen with the more overtly aversive yet highly responsive and reactive controlling caregivers. Up to a point, it is better to respond badly than to be nonresponsive. Reconstructive clinical histories generally bear out this impression, as does Spitz's and Bowlby's work on children in orphanages. Contingency itself, irrespective of hedonic value, is a potent and all-pervasive element at the very heart of relatedness.

In the face of overstimulation, especially where the caregiver is insensitive, we have frequently seen infants utilizing a different "technique" of adapting to the misregulated system. They become glassy eyed and stare right through or just past the caregiver's face. Spitz has pointed out that almost all infants do this at times. Yet this behavior continues to intrigue me. Could it be a very early and partial form of dissociating or splitting off the perception from the internal feeling state related to that perception? When the infant goes into one of these stares I assume that he refocuses his eyes at some point infinitely far away. Nonetheless his eyes rest on the caregiver's face so that form perception of her facial behavior is probably being registered but unattended. The infant is thus potentially capable of perceiving exactly what the caregiver is doing, but his visual attention on the stimulus events she provides has been attenuated enough so that these events no longer appear to influence his internal states of excitation or affect.

This infant behavior has the flavor of tuning out but in a relatively acceptable way. I followed one infant of a fairly insensitive and overstimulating mother who by four months of age was a master at this particular form of partial inattention. I saw him through his second year, and he developed into a quite normal little boy, a touch low-keyed but not without the ability to become engagingly animated. Still he maintained the tendency or ability to make you feel that he was not continually and consistently "there" for you, but had momentarily gone or escaped to somewhere else. This phenomenon did not appear in any way to be a sign of pathology in him. It had more the quality of what it was like to be with this particular person. Nonetheless, the complex psychic and behavioral operation we are looking at has clear potential for evolving into later maladaptive coping or defensive operations if life's pressures so channel it.

Going limp, or otherwise inhibiting motility, is another infant behavior of considerable interest when performed in the face of an overstimulating interaction. Beebe describes this well in a frame-by-frame analysis of a mother-infant interaction in which the chase and dodge game is overzealously pursued by the mother. After several attempts at gaze aversion, emotional signaling with facial expressions, and physical escape all fail, the infant goes limp for a moment or so. We have seen this momentary inhibition in many infants, often accompanied by staring. In some, however, it appears to become a more predominant and chronic means of dealing with overstimulation.

Once again the speculative implications are far-reaching. When one considers that the motor apparatus over which the four-month-old infant has voluntary control consists mainly of the eyes, face, head, and some not too well coordinated arm and leg movements, the simple act of going limp represents a massive inhibition of his executive functioning (or motor ego functions). Here too the question arises whether we are watching the origins of a behavior that under pressure of the "right" or "wrong" dyadic and life circumstances will later develop into maladaptive motor inhibitions or passivity as a reaction to interpersonal stress.

Finally, there is the unusual infant who is exceptionally sensitive to stimuli or, put differently, has a lower threshold and an optimal range that is absolutely lower though perhaps of the same width. It is hard for a normally behaving caregiver not to overstimulate such an infant, and she must modulate her behavior. The "problem" may be more complicated than having a lower threshold for stimulation (which may be relatively selective to one sensory modality, such as hearing). Such an infant may also be less well able to tolerate a rapid acceleration in the intensity of a stimulus and the concomitant level of internal excitement. The same rising stimulus that would make one infant smile would be too intense for this infant, and he might cry. Even if the stimulus burst were in the right optimal range, its rate of acceleration might be overwhelming.

Periodically, theories appear suggesting that many infants

who are born with constitutionally high sensitivities to most stimuli must evolve adaptations that will protect them from the barrage of stimulus events, especially the highly stimulating human events, that they experience. The more extreme adaptations result in the severely protective and withdrawing behaviors that are synonymous with childhood autism. These theories and their variations have yet to be proved or disproved. Indeed a small number of children who become autistic give retrospective histories of extreme sensitivity to most and especially human stimuli during infancy. Nonetheless, the vast majority of hypersensitive infants either beome less so as development proceeds or grow up to become normal children and adults with a lower threshold to stimuli and often with more finely tuned sensibilities, which may or may not be put to creative use.

REGULATORY FAILURES AND UNDERSTIMULATION

Any dyadic condition that prevents the capturing and holding of attention, or allows the level of excitation and affect to fall or remain below the lower boundary of an optimal range, can be called a condition of understimulation. The reasons for such a dyadic condition can be extremely diverse both in origin and in reversibility. On the mother's side, the reasons consist mainly of disturbances in the ability to perform effective infant-elicited social behaviors.

If a mother is depressed, for example, she may be able to go through all the practical activities of caregiving, but she will not be able to light up her face or voice or movements. The necessary envelopes of stimulus intensity and contour that are so well designed to influence the infant's attention, excitement, and affect will be unavailable to her. The progressively rising and climaxing stimulus bursts needed to generate the arousal jags that produce affect will be missing; so will the rapid shifts in pitch or speed or modality to recapture a flagging attention; and so will the suspenseful stretching of tempo and other surprising shifts in timing. The depressed caregiver will be unable to play with her own behavior in order to play with her infant.

Similarly, a mother with restricted or flattened emotional responses because of a schizophrenic process will have a limited range and reduced ability to modulate the intensity and richness of the social stimuli she provides for the infant. A caregiver who, for characterological or neurotic reasons, has an excessive inhibition of spontaneity will be in a roughly similar position. (However, we have often seen caregivers who are quite inhibited in most of their adult interactions come to life with their infants.)

Understimulation may also occur with a caregiver who has an entirely normal repertoire of infant-elicited social behaviors, but there is an interference with the eliciting power of the infant upon her, even though the infant is by all standards a quite adequate eliciting stimulus. If the caregiver is obsessively preoccupied with thoughts unrelated to the baby, or if she is resentful and rejecting of her baby or the caregiving role, then she may be relatively impervious or insensitive to her infant's invitations, and little will be forthcoming from her in the way of infant-elicited social behaviors, even though she has a fully available but latent repertoire. Once again, understimulation will prevail.*

We have seen understimulation result by yet another pathway. Some caregivers are oversensitive to or fearful of rejection from their infants. Sometimes this insecurity is limited to their caregiving role, but just as often it is a manifestation of a more pervasive insecurity. In either event, this often gets played out by the caregiver who acts as if each termination of infant attention, each gaze aversion, were a "micro-rejection" and each return of gaze a "micro-acceptance." Feeling rejected, the caregiver interprets an infant gaze aversion as a permanent cut-off behavior and stops the interaction by getting up and walking away or putting the infant down, instead of seeing the aversion as a temporary holding and readjusting behavior. Accordingly, play sessions frequently get terminated too quickly, long before the infant is ready to stop. The result is that the duration of stimulation falls short of the infant's capacity.

A similar "short-fall" of stimulation happens if the caregiver has a limited stereotyped repertoire of variations of social behavior. Some fathers or other family members who interact little with their infants demonstrate this situation in caricature. When a stereotypic father comes home after work and he and the infant

*In all of these situations it is worth imagining what the infant's predominant sensori-motor-affective experiences are likely to be, since they will become internalized to form representations of his first and foremost relationship.

are ready to play, he runs through his repertoire. First he plays "bounce on the knee" with great delight for both. When the baby slowly habituates to that stimulus, he shifts to "wagging heads side to side together," and after that begins to pall he switches to "tickle the tummy." In all three games he is a marvelously rich source of stimulation and conducts the transitions from one game to the next with great sensitivity to the infant's trend and drift. However, after "tickle the tummy" has run its course for the infant, the father has exhausted his entire repertoire of stereotyped games. He then terminates the interaction; while the infant may have tired of the last game, he is nonetheless ready for a new and different one. Unfortunately, the father has none available.

A somewhat analogous situation may occur when a caregiver is very inhibited or even phobic, for whatever reason, in any one modality of play, most usually in touching or providing vigorous kinesthetic stimulation. In these circumstances the interaction may run smoothly and beautifully through many episodes of richly and variously combined vocal and facial behaviors. At some point, however, something different and more vigorous may be needed to maintain the flow, such as a switch to proximal stimulation through touching or bouncing. But the caregiver cannot provide it and the interactive flow begins to ebb.

So far I have mentioned only the caregiver as the initial source of misregulation. The primary event may also reside in the infant's behavior. If the infant is hypoactive or has a significant developmental lag or minimal brain damage, then a normally effective amount of stimulation may not move him up to or keep him within the optimal range. At the same time, he will be unable to produce the smiles and coos and other actions that evoke infant-elicited social behaviors from the caregiver. The caregiver is then put in the bind of not being adequately stimulated by the baby to produce the behaviors that will adequately stimulate him to provide the eliciting behaviors that will stimulate her to stimulate him to . . . and so on. Even when the caregiver can get herself going on her own, often by dint of much effort, her efforts may be insufficient to stimulate that baby and cannot be maintained except with considerable determination, which is exhausting and unrewarding. In such a situation, to keep the dyadic interaction mutually regulated, the caregiver has to readjust her own behavioral repertoire and stimulus level to match the infant's range of responsivity. She also has to "retrain" herself to find what social behaviors are available to the infant and responsive to her behavior. This is no easy task. However, to the extent it can be accomplished, a mutually regulating dyadic system can be restored with all of the advantages that this carries for the infant's social and cognitive development.

REGULATORY FAILURES AND PARADOXICAL STIMULATION

We have seen a handful of mothers who only come to life for their infants to provide effective stimulus events when their infants hurt themselves or have some other discomforting mishap. This is an unusual and happily infrequent form of selective paradoxical responsivity. These mothers were all extremely ambivalent about their infants and closely approached the degree of disturbance in their caregiving that could classify them as "neglecting" or "abusive" mothers. (The two go together more frequently then not.) These mothers were generally quite deadpan when faced with their infants and seemed to engage little in social play, let alone animated play.

All infants have a "repertoire" of common self-hurtful or discomforting mishaps, such as losing their balance in the chair and falling "slow motion" to one side; or missing their mouth with a spoonful and landing the stuff in the eye, ear, or chin; or misjudging a reach for something and falling forward on their face; or miscalculating the trajectory of an object they are bringing toward their face and bumping it against their forehead. Many of these misoccurences are in fact funny in the way that slapstick is funny, and most caregivers may laugh (if there is no real injury) and also give some soothing "there-there" behaviors.

What is unusual about this group of mothers is that only when one of these mishaps befalls the infant do they come alive. Only when inspired by the "funny" circumstances of the infant's discomfort does the mother perform lively infant-elicited social behaviors. At those moments she shifts from her deadpan uninvolvement and becomes an effective social partner. At that point, the infant usually rapidly recovers from his mishap in response to his "transformed" mother, and they then share one of their rare moments of mutually pleasurable and exciting stimulation. The problem of course is that the infant's main moments of interactive delight and liveliness with his mother are dependent upon and perhaps become associated with an immediately preceding unpleasurable feeling. A more ideal learning paradigm could hardly be devised for acquiring the basis of masochism: pain as the condition and prerequisite for pleasure. (The maternal behavior of these mothers is not without obvious sadism.)

Though the "average" mother may also become amused, involved, and animated at these minor mishaps, her infant-elicited social behaviors are evoked by such a wide range of other more frequent behaviors, as well as spontaneously produced, that any association between the discomfort and the subsequent pleasure would be washed away.

Another far more common form of paradoxical stimulation consists of expending enormous amounts of time, energy, and sensitivity on another person while avoiding full contact and, at the same time, full disengagement. As casual students of human behavior we have all seen many versions of the intricate interpersonal choreography that allows people to miss the chances to really get together and yet also avoid the opportunities to really get apart. It can occur between couples, or parents and children, or friends. The mutual sensitivity lies in assuring the "misses" and securing the "bind."

One version of this might be called the mutual approach-withdrawal dance. I have previously analyzed in detail the intricate steps that perpetuate one variation of this pattern.[4] It went like this.

The mother was a committed and caring woman who gave birth to twins, Mark and Fred. As has commonly been observed in mothers of twins, some of the "normal" ambivalence about having twins is split so that more of the positive feelings are initially attached to one baby and more of the negative feelings to the other. This is not unusual and generally corrects itself after a while. In this particular case, the mother had already made distinctions between the twins while they were still in her womb. One baby kicked more and, because the mother thought of herself as a lively and energetic person, she made a closer identification with that active yet unseen presence. After delivery, she somehow assumed that Mark, who really was the more active infant of the two, was the one who had been kicking more inside. In any event, this mother found things easier with Mark, and she experienced a more ready rapport with him. The interaction and the rapport were harder and more turbulent with Fred, the quiet child.

The particular play session used for detailed frame-by-frame film analysis was chosen because it was highly characteristic of most of their social interactions. Mother sat on the floor with each infant (they were three-and-a half months old) placed in separate infant seats in front of her. The play, as usual, went effortlessly with Mark and got progressively worse with Fred until his fussiness terminated the period. I wanted to know what was so different about the two interactions: mother with Mark and mother with Fred. To do this the film was viewed frame by frame through a movie editor. A number was printed on each frame. In this way I could move the film forward or backward as many times as I wanted, and as fast or slow as I needed to record what happened in each frame.*

The first phenomenon this method made apparent was that mother and Fred tended to move almost exactly together, like two puppets on the same set of strings. Furthermore, their movements followed a clear pattern. When mother approached Fred

*For those readers who are interested in the fine-grained analysis of behavior, there is something I want to say about this method of analysis. It brings the researcher into very intimate contact with the material. Much as I became involved with the process between Jenny and her mother, so through this method did I become a participant-observer of the interaction between the twins and their mother. The method is used less now because technological advances in both TV and film equipment have made a variety of playback features available: stop frames, forward and backward slow-motion capabilities, etc., all at the flip of a switch. Something gets lost with these innovations, however. Using the old editor and hand-operated take-up reels to view a single complete behavior from boundary to boundary, from start to finish, you have to rotate the reels with both arms, one hand on each, from exactly "here" to exactly "there" to get the entire movement under scrutiny. After watching that single behavior, say the crescendo and decrescendo of a mother's smile, over and over, your spatial coordination becomes perfected so that you can start and stop the film exactly at the boundaries of the behavior. You have then become a participant-observer. You can reproduce the stretch of the mother's behavior even with your eyes closed because the "knowledge" of where the boundaries are now resides in

he withdrew, and when Fred approached mother she withdrew. This pattern is illustrated in Figure 8, drawn from the film.

This was the first time it became obvious that a mother and infant could move together and start and stop moving together, at least for short stretches, with the kind of precision that argued for the model of a shared program rather than a stimulus-response explanation. To assure myself that much of this "dancing together" actually occurred, I covered up one half of the screen and recorded at what point the mother started an approach toward or a withdrawal from Fred. I then did the reverse, recording in which frames Fred started an approach toward or a withdrawal from mother. When I compared these two records it became apparent that most of the time the two were acting simultaneously for all purposes. Sometimes, however, one member would start to move, or stop, long enough before the other, so that one movement could be considered a stimulus and the other a response. In these cases mother was slightly more often the leader.

It turned out that Mark too was moving roughly synchronously with mother's movements, but only when they were facing and looking at one another during an interaction. Otherwise Mark's movements were independent of mother's. Fred, on the other hand, continued to move with mother, even when she was not looking at or interacting with him, and even when he was not looking directly at her. He was apparently always monitoring her movements peripherally and responding to them with his own movements. In this sense, he always remained in responsive contact with her; it was never broken. But Mark was in responsive contact with her only when they were also engaged in mutual gaze; otherwise he broke contact.

Another crucial difference in the two interactions was that mother acted differently toward a gaze aversion depending on

---

your own arms and hands. This intimate involvement with the data allows a rare opportunity. While you reproduce the single maternal behavior "with your arms," you can now watch the infant with your eyes, but knowing all the time when the mother is doing what. In a sense, by letting your body become part of the action, it becomes "trained" to do one observational task while your eyes are left free to do another. And only both together tell the whole story.

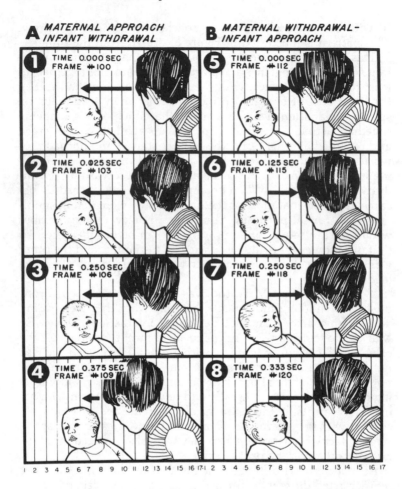

A *MATERNAL APPROACH INFANT WITHDRAWAL* **B** *MATERNAL WITHDRAWAL– INFANT APPROACH*

8. *Mutual approach-withdrawal pattern between a mother and one of her 3½-month-old twins, drawn from my film.*

who performed it. If Mark averted his face, the mother accepted this as a temporary cut-off and either looked away or sat still. If Fred averted his face, mother did not accept it as a cut-off signal and moved closer toward him as if to force a fuller contact but succeeding only in forcing him into a position of greater aversion.

In summary, the pattern of steps between Fred and mother traced a repeating sequence that went as follows: If Fred and mother are facing one another in a moment of mutual gaze, a moment of usually short duration between them, Fred would invariably avert his gaze slightly *as* mother moved toward him. Instead of considering Fred's face aversion as a signal to back off (as she does with Mark), she treats it as a signal to approach closer. One reason she may act differently with Fred is that, unlike Mark, even when Fred averts his gaze he continues to monitor her every move, and she may sense this through the responsivity of his movements to hers. This may give her the impression that he is still in contact with her, so she moves closer to establish full face-to-face and eye contact. This sends Fred even farther away into an exaggerated face aversion. From that position *as* Fred turns back toward her, she withdraws and turns away. It is still a mutual approach-withdrawal flow but now in the other direction, Fred approaching and mother withdrawing. By the time she is fully withdrawn and facing away from Fred, he is now fully facing her again and still executing the small approach and withdrawal movements that are dependent on her motions toward him, even though her motions are no longer related to him. She is looking elsewhere. However, the combination of his gazing at her and moving with her quickly recaptures her attention. She again turns to Fred, and as she moves toward him he averts and they are again retracing the same sequential steps.

One of the striking features of this pattern of "missing" is that mother and Fred never got together fully for long, and never stay completely apart for long. Yet they spend much more time and effort working or rather failing at getting together. (Mark and mother spend less time interacting but more time in mutual gaze and face-to-face contact.)

One of the interesting outcomes of this interactive pattern was that through the second year of life Fred continued to have more trouble in both establishing and maintaining mutual gaze with mother and others, compared to Mark, and also more trouble in disengaging from mother and wandering off alone without checking back, as did Mark. In general he remained less attached and less separated.

One of the main inferences from this example of paradoxical stimulation is that the course of the separation-individuation phase of development, which becomes a major developmental issue in the second year of life, may be partially foreshadowed and predetermined by the interactive patterns established in the first half year of life, when the major developmental issue is attachment.

Attachment and separation, or engagement and disengagement, are inextricably related, opposite sides of the same coin. Generally when viewing infants in the first year, we focus on the attachment aspect and, when viewing them in the second year, on the separation-individuation aspect. This is a somewhat artificial and potentially misleading, though comprehensible, shift in focus. During the first year of life the attachment behaviors are coming into full bloom. Smiling, gazing, clinging, and cooing are the forms that seem to fill the picture, while gaze aversions, stares, and momentary inhibitions make up the space between the forms. Then in the second year the separation behaviors appear to bloom, and mobility, walking away and getting involved with objects, become the form that fill out the picture while the gaze back at mother and the periodic vocalizations now fill the spaces.

The point is that the entire "picture" at either age consists of the relationship between the dominant forms and the shapes of the spaces in between them. The structure and function of engagement and disengagement are interlocked so that the developmental history of one must encompass the developmental history of the other, regardless of which phase of development the child is in. The beginnings of separation and individuation must be cotemporaneous with the beginnings of attachment.

9 / Finding Your Own Path

It is quite obvious that when an infant is "deviant" or a mother's behavior abnormal and obviously deleterious, we have to intervene immediately with whatever knowledge and ingenuity are available and likely to be helpful. But all of us, caregivers, researchers, educators, and clinicians, are now in a different position, a transitional place. We are greatly encouraged and excited by our rapidly growing understanding of the biology and psychology of the infant's social development, yet not able fully to translate this knowledge into day-to-day practice. Working at this point of transition poses problems about knowing what is normal and what is abnormal and what, if anything, to do about it. Intervention, even educational intervention, is always problematic, and restraint is called for in face of the zeal created by our new knowledge.

First of all, we simply do not yet know our own cultural range of normal infant-caregiver interactive patterns. An intervention implies that something identifiable is wrong. The distinction is not always clear (in the minds of observers with similar training and often similar backgrounds) between potential pathological patterns and simply "the way things are" in any given family. After all, the infant is in part being shaped to grow up, live, and fit in with that caregiver in that setting. Erik Erikson has made us all aware how each society raises its children so that they will make an adaptive fit with the needs and nature of that particular society. The same is true within each family.

Second, even when most of us can agree that something looks amiss in an interaction, we do not know with sufficient surety if it will correct itself in a month, or in the next phase of development, or if it doesn't, what its long-range consequences will be. Without that surety, interventions are not justifiable.

Third, even if we were more certain about what to tell a caregiver and could say "do this, not that," the cure might be worse than the disease. One of the most effective features of a caregiver's social behavior is its spontaneity. In fact, the ability to perform effective infant-elicited variations of social behavior rests to a large extent on a base of unselfconsciousness and an intuituve trust in your own behavior. To impair this might put at risk one of the caregiver's most potent assets and place different strains and stresses on the interactive fit.

The same problems that encumber the issue of intervention surround aspects of education for caregiving. Yet education in some form is sorely needed. From working with caregivers, mostly first-time mothers, I have seen how most of them really "learn their trade." It's not through any of the medical, paramedical, or educational institutions. If a woman does not live in an extended family, and most no longer do, she learns through informal groupings of caregivers. These small and transient yet powerful and ubiquitous floating "institutions" are the vitally important disseminators of information. They are usually formed haphazardly by who lives on your block, or in your building, or who your sister knows, or who you met in the playground and happens to have an infant roughly your infant's age, or a little older, if you are lucky, since she has been there already last month.

It is in these loosely structured, informal social groupings that much of the real education and needed emotional support for the "job" occurs, not in our recognized institutions and not through how-to books. I suspect that being a primary caregiver is more like being a creative artist than anything else, performing in your own work as you create it: a choreographer-dancer or a composer-musician. Note that I have stressed the nonverbal, temporally dynamic arts, at least during this period of infancy.

The cultural norms will seep in anyway, and formal training is useful and invaluable but only for mastering basic technical skills such as diapering, bathing, nutrition, and feeding. However, the process of having a social interaction and playing with an infant cannot really be taught. That does not mean that the caregiver cannot learn more and more about this process, find it easier to create and perform in, and enjoy it more thereby.

The process of learning to interact with an infant and getting the "feel" of the interactive process is roughly similar from one caregiver to the next, but with some real differences too. Still for each caregiver, subjectively, it feels as if the events and emotions she encounters are highly personal and individual to her and her baby, exclusively and unsharably so. Creating and performing in a continually improvised and often idiosyncratic social interaction can be a lonely, even alienating process. No one has ever written down the "steps and notes" to be followed, since they are improvised as you go, and no one has ever listed or "sanctioned" the wide variety of new, often unusual, and unexpected behavioral combinations a caregiver will unwittingly find herself using with her infant. At some point, then, most caregivers find or feel themselves to be out alone on a limb of improvised behavioral interactions of their own personal creation. To some this experience is exhilarating, to more it is often frightening.

I assume that all creative ventures, of which daily social interaction with an infant is one, periodically come to that lonely place where both the path that has been taken and everything you are now doing is questioned. It is for this reason that I believe that any consciousness-raising peer group of caregivers is the best educational "device" to impart new ideas, emotional support, and, perhaps most important, the perspective that what each is doing and worrying about is generally quite common and shared by all, to know, in other words, that every good mother is out on her own limb.

It is also the same reason that this book was written. In this spirit, I have tried to share information, so that a caregiver can create the steps of her own unique "dance" with her infant and at the same time know that the individual "movements" she and they make, and the improvised sequences they trace, are even in their individuality part of a natural process common to us all.

The first general lesson that has come from these studies is that the conduct of social interaction, even with an infant, is an individual and intricate process: of improvising on-the-spot unexpected behaviors that come from within; of spontaneously creating and changing temporal patterns and behavioral sequences that have never been performed exactly like that before and yet are seen a million times over; of flexibly altering pitch and tone and speed and modality unthinkingly as you go along, on the basis of cues that flash by and are only vaguely experienced and partially identified, but enough perceived to lead to a new and unknown direction of action; but all this within the solid structured framework that nature has provided both infant and caregiver.

The other major lesson is that this system of variability within structure is one to which both infant and caregiver bring the necessary behaviors and responsivities so that it is set to "run" with the surety and robustness that reflect the work of nature's gradual perfecting over several millennia of evolution an interactive system designed to develop individuals, not mistakes.

References
Suggested Reading
Index

References

2 The Caregiver's Repertoire

1. I. Eibl-Eibesfeldt, *Ethology, the Biology of Behavior* (New York: Holt, Rinehart and Winston, 1970). A. Kendon and A. Ferber, "A Description of Some Human Greetings." In R.P. Michael and J.H. Crook, eds., *Comparative Ecology and Behavior of Primates* (London: Academic Press, 1973).

2. C. A. Ferguson, "Baby Talk in Six Languages." In J. Gumperz and D. Hymes, eds., *The Ethnography of Communication*, 1964, *66*, 103-114.

3. K. Nelson, "Structure and Strategy in Learning To Talk," *Monograph of the Society for Research in Child Development*, 1973, *38*, (102, serial no. 149).

4. C. Snow, "Mother's Speech to Children Learning Language," *Child Development*, 1972, *43*, 549-564. D. Stern, "Mother and Infant at Play: The Dyadic Interaction Involving Facial, Vocal and Gaze Behaviors." In M. Lewis and L. Rosenblum, eds., *The Effect of the Infant on Its Caregiver* (New York: Wiley, 1974). D. Slobin, "On the Nature of Talk to Children." In E. Lenneberg and E. Lenneberg, eds., *Foundations of Language Development, I* (New York: Academic Press, 1975).

5. D. Stern and J. Jaffe, "Dialogic Vocal Patterns Between Mothers and Infant." Paper presented at the Conference on Interaction, Conversation and the Development of Language. Educational Testing Service, Princeton, October 1976.

6. M.C. Bateson, "Mother-Infant Exchanges: The Epigenesis of Conversational Interaction," *Annals of the New York Academy of Sciences*, 1975, *263*, 101-113.

7. D. Stern, J. Jaffe, B. Beebe, and S.L. Bennett, "Vocalizing in Unison and in Alternation: Two Modes of Communication Within the Mother-Infant Dyad," *Annals of the New York Academy of Sciences*, 1975, *263*, 89-100.

8. H.R. Schaffer, G.M. Collis, and G. Parsons, "Vocal Interchange and Visual Regard in Verbal and Pre-Verbal Children." In H.R. Schaffer, ed., *Studies on Mother-Infant Interaction* (New York and London: Academic Press, 1977).

9. M. Argyle and A. Kendon, "The Experimental Analysis of Social Performance." In L. Berkowitz, ed., *Advances in Experimental Social Psychology*, vol. 3 (New York: Academic Press, 1967). A.

138 / References

Kendon, "Some Functions of Gaze Direction in Social Interactions," *Acta Psychologica*, 1967, *26*, 22-63.

10. J.C. Peery and D. Stern, "Gaze Duration Frequency Distributions During Mother-Infant Interactions," *Journal of Genetic Psychology*, 1976, *129*, 45-55.

11. T.G.R. Bower, "Stimulus Variables Determining Space Perception in Infants," *Science*, 1965, *149*, 88-89.

12. E. Tronick, L. Adamson, S. Wise, H. Als, and T.B. Brazelton, "The Infant's Response to Entrapment Between Contradictory Messages in Face to Face Interaction." Paper presented at the Society for Research in Child Development, Denver, March 1975.

13. E. Aronson and S. Rosenbloom, "Space Perception in Early Infancy: Perception Within a Common Auditory-Visual Space," *Science*, 1971, *172*, 1161-1163.

14. W. Fullard and A.M. Rieling, "An Investigation of Lorenz's 'Babyness,' " *Child Development*, 1976, *47*, 1191-1193.

15. I. DeVore and M.J. Konner, "Infancy in Hunter-Gatherer Life: An Ethological Perspective." In White, ed., *Ethology and Psychiatry*. See also I. DeVore and R.B. Lee, eds., *Kalahari Hunter-Gatherers* (Cambridge: Harvard University Press, 1976).

3 The Infant's Repertoire

1. M. von Senden, *Space and Sight*, trans. P. Heath (Glencoe, Ill.: Free Press, 1960). A discussion of Von Senden's work can be found in R.A. Spitz and W.G. Coblinger, *The First Year of Life* (New York: International Universities Press, 1966).

2. K.S. Robson, "The Role of Eye to Eye Contact in Maternal-Infant Attachment," *Journal of Child Psychology and Psychiatry*, 1967, *8*, 13-25.

3. R. Ahrens, "Beitrag zur Entwicklung des Physiognomie-und Mimikerkennens," *Z. Exp. Angew. Psychol.*, 1954, *2*, 412-454. R.A. Spitz and K.M. Wolf, "The Smiling Response: A Contribution to the Ontogenesis of Social Relations," *Genet. Psychol. Monogr.*, 1946, *34*, 57-125.

4. R.L. Fantz, "Visual Experience in Infants: Decreased Attention to Familiar Patterns Relative to Novel Ones," *Science*, 1964, *146*, 668-670.

5. D. Freedman, "Smiling in Blind Infants and the Issue of Innate vs. Acquired," *Journal of Child Psychology and Psychiatry*, 1964, 5, 171-184. R.A. Haaf and R.Q. Bell, "A Facial Dimension in Visual Discrimination by Human Infants," *Child Development*, 1967, *38*, 893-899.

6. P.H. Wolff, "Observations on the Early Development of Smiling." In B.M. Foss, ed., *Determinants of Infant Behavior*, vol. 2 (New York: Wiley, 1963).

7. B. Beebe and D. Stern, "Engagement-Disengagement and Early Object Experiences." In N. Freedman and S. Grand, eds., *Communicative Structures and Psychic Structures* (New York: Plenum, 1977, forthcoming).

8. D. Stern, "Mother and Infant at Play: The Dyadic Interaction Involving Facial, Vocal and Gaze Behaviors." In M. Lewis and L. Rosenblum, eds., *The Effect of the Infant on Its Caregiver* (New York: Wiley, 1974).

9. W.R. Charlesworth and M. Kreutzer, "Facial Expressions of Infants and Children." In P. Ekman, ed., *Darwin and Facial Expression* (New York: Academic Press, 1973).

10. S.L. Bennett, "Infant-Caretaker Interactions," *Journal of the American Academy of Child Psychiatry*, 1971, *10*, 321-335.

11. R. Emde, T. Gaensbauer, and R. Harmon, "Emotional Expression in Infancy: A Biobehavioral Study," *Psychological Issues Monograph Series*, 1976, *10*, 1, No. 37.

12. L.A. Sroufe and E. Waters, "The Ontogenesis of Smiling and Laughter: A Perspective on the Organization of Development in Infancy," *Psychological Review*, 1976, *83*, 173-189.

4 From Laboratory to Real Life

1. J.S. Bruner, "The Ontogenesis of Speech Acts," *Journal of Child Language*, 1975, *2*, 1-19.

2. R.M. Yerkes and J.D. Dodson, "The Relation of Strength of Stimulus to Rapidity of Habit-Formation," *J. Comp. Neurol. Psychol.*, 1908, *18*, 458-482. J. Kagan and M. Lewis, "Studies on Attention in the Human Infant," *Merrill-Palmer Quarterly*, 1965, *11*, 95-127.

3. M. Lewis, S. Goldberg, and H. Campbell, "A Developmental Study of Learning Within the First Three Years of Life: Response Decrement to a Redundant Signal," *Society for Research in Child Development Monographs*, 1969, *34*, 9, No. 133.

4. J. Kagan, "Stimulus-Schema Discrepancy and Attention in the Infant," *Journal of Experimental Child Psychology*, 1967, *5*, 381-390.

5. J.I. Lacey, "Somatic Response Patterning and Stress: Some Versions of Activation Theory." *American Handbook of Psychiatry*, vol. 4 (New York: Basic Books, 1974).

6. R.B. McCall and J. Kagan, "Attention in the Infant: Effects of Complexity, Contour, Perimeter, and Familiarity," *Child Development*, 1967, *38*, 939-952. G. Stechler and G. Carpenter, "A Viewpoint on Early Affective Development." In J. Hellmuth, ed., *The Exceptional Infant*, vol. 1 (Seattle: Special Child Publications, 1967).

7. D.E. Berlyne, "Laughter, Humor and Play." In G. Lindzey and A.

Aronson, eds., *Handbook of Social Psychology*, vol. 3 (Boston: Addison-Wesley, 1969).

8. J. Kagan, *Change and Continuity in Infancy* (New York: Wiley, 1971).

6 Structure and Timing

1. A. Fogel, "Tempo Organization in Mother-Infant Face to Face Interaction." In H.R. Schaffer, ed., *Studies on Mother-Infant Interaction* (London: Academic Press, 1977).
2. C. Snow, "Mother's Speech to Children Learning Language," *Child Development*, 1972, *43*, 549-564.
3. B. Beebe, "Ontogeny of Positive Affect in the Third and Fourth Months of the Life of One Infant." PhD dissertation, Columbia University, University Microfilms, 1973.
4. A.B. Kristofferson, "Low Variance Stimulus Response Latencies: Deterministic Internal Delays," *Perception and Psychophysics*, 1976, *20*, 89-100.
5. W.J. McGill, "Neural Counting Mechanisms and Energy Detection in Audition," *Journal of Mathematical Psychology*, 1967, *4*, 351-376. D.J. Getty, "Discrimination of Short Temporal Intervals: A Comparison of Two Models," *Perception and Psychophysics*, 1975, *18*, 1-8. J. Gibbon, "Scalar Expectancy Theory and Weber's Law in Animal Timing," *Psychological Review*, 1977, forthcoming.
6. D. Stern and J. Gibbon, "Temporal Expectancies of Social Behaviors in Mother-Infant Play." In E. Thorman, ed., *The Origins of the Infant's Responsiveness* (New York: L. Erhlbaum Press, 1977, forthcoming).

7 From Interaction to Relationship

1. See M. Lewis and L. Rosenblum, eds., *The Origins of Fear* (New York: Wiley, 1974).
2. T.B. Brazelton, B. Koslowski, and M. Main, "The Origins of Reciprocity: The Early Mother-Infant Interaction." In M. Lewis and L. Rosenblum, eds., *The Effect of the Infant on Its Caregiver* (New York: Wiley, 1974).
3. S.M. Bell, "The Development of the Concept of the Object as Related to Infant-Mother Attachment," *Child Development*, 1970, *41*, 291-311.
4. W.R. Charlesworth and M. Kreutzer, "Facial Expressions of Infants and Children." In P. Ekman, ed., *Darwin and Facial Expression* (New York: Academic Press, 1973).
5. M. Mahler and M. Furer, *On Human Symbiosis and the Vicissi-*

tudes of Individuation (New York: International Universities Press, 1968).

8 Missteps in the Dance

1. A. Thomas, H.G. Birch, S. Chess, M.E. Hertzig, and S. Korn, *Behavioral Individuality in Early Childhood* (New York: New York University Press, 1963).
2. C. Hutt and C. Ounsted, "The Biological Significance of Gaze Aversion with Particular Reference to the Syndrome of Infantile Autism," *Behavioral Science*, 1966, *11*, 346-356.
3. B. White, *Human Infants: Experience and Psychological Development* (Englewood Cliffs, N.J.: Prentice-Hall, 1971).
4. D.N. Stern, "A Micro-Analysis of Mother-Infant Interaction: Behavior Regulating Social Contact Between a Mother and Her 3½-month-old Twins," *Journal of the American Academy of Child Psychiatry*, 1971, *10*, 501-517.

Suggested Reading

Konrad Z. Lorenz, *King Solomon's Ring* (New York: Crowell, 1952). Much of my own thinking and seeing, as well as that of many others interested in infants, has been greatly influenced by ethological work on animal behavior. As a first introduction to this important perspective, Lorenz's delightful personal account of his experiences and relationships with the animals he observes is ideal.

Robert A. Hinde, *Biological Basis of Human Social Behavior* (New York: McGraw-Hill, 1974). If *King Solomon's Ring* stimulates further curiosity about animal behavior and especially its potential implications for human behavior, Hinde's book is a next step. It is an excellent overview of ethological studies and theories of those aspects of animal behavior that clearly have the greatest relevance for an understanding of humans.

John Bowlby, *Attachment and Loss, I: Attachment* (London: Hogarth Press, 1968; New York: Basic Books, 1969). Bowlby combines an ethological perspective with vast clinical psychiatric experience and brings both to focus upon an examination of the nature of the child's tie to his mother. The resultant theoretical formulation of attachment has contributed much to current psychological and psychoanalytic thinking, has stimulated new approaches to the study of early human social development, and has altered many of our attitudes about early child care.

A. Thomas, S. Chess, H. Birch, H. Hertzig, and S. Korn, *Behavioral Individuality in Early Childhood* (New York: New York University Press, 1963).

Sibylle K. Escalona, *The Roots of Individuality* (Chicago: Aldine, 1968).

T. Berry Brazelton, *Infants and Mothers: Differences in Development* (New York: Dell, 1969).

These three books have a common theme, the nature and development of individual differences in children. The first extensively documents and examines individual differences in temperment and their implications for development. Escalona's book focuses more on the nature of various interactional fits between different infants and different caregiving environments. Brazelton's book is written mainly for mothers. He uses his rich pediatric and research experience to trace the developmental course during the first year of three normal infants—an "average," a quiet, and an active baby.

Burton White, *The First Three Years of Life* (Englewood Cliffs, N.J.: Prentice-Hall, 1975). This book presents in a clear, readily understandable fashion our current state of knowledge about the infant's perceptual and cognitive capabilities and their developmental course. If the reader wishes a more detailed account of these processes, written for the infant researcher, he should see Leslie Cohen and Philip Salapatek, *Infant Perception: From Sensation to Cognition, II: Perception of Space, Speech and Sound* (New York: Academic Press, 1975).

Eveoleen N. Rexford, Louis W. Sander, and Theodore Shapiro, eds., *Infant Psychiatry: A New Synthesis* (New Haven and London: Yale University Press, 1976). The explosion of knowledge about the infant has in a sense created a new field, infant psychiatry. This collection of papers brings together a number of contributions on how our expanded understanding can be related to pathological and potentially pathological developmental situations in infancy.

Index

Absolute Timing, 89

Affect: Freud on, 64-65; related to tension and release, 65; direction of, 66; motor expression of as communication, 116

Affective experience: in representations, 99, 103-104; "uncoupling" of, 106

Affiliative behavior, 95

Ahrens, R., 36

Attention: and stimulation, 54-61; level of stimulation, 54-56; shut-off point, 56-57; repetitious stimulation, 56-58; effect of discrepancy, 60

Avoidance behavior: by closing the eyes, 38; by turning the head, 41; by lowering the head, 41-42; as signal of overstimulation, 110-114

Baby talk, character of, 14-15

"Babyness," 24-26

Bateson, M. Catherine, 17

Bell, Richard Q., 37

Bell, Sylvia, 97

Bennett, Stephen L., 43-44

Berlyne, D. E., 65

Bloom, Lois, 15

Body movements, of infant, as process units in motor experience, 102

Bowlby, John, 117

Brazelton, T. Berry, 97

Bruner, Jerome S., 53-54

Caregiver: facial expressions of, 11-14; vocalizations, 14-18; gaze, 18-19; face presentations, 19-20;

proxemics, 20-21; integration of stimuli by, 22-23; reasons for elicitation of special behavior by, 23-30; primary and secondary, 109; overstimulation by, 115-119; understimulation by, 119-122

Charlesworth, William R., 43

Children, ages of related to caregiver's actions, 26-27

Cognitive stimulation: beginning of, 52-53; infant's pursuit of, 53-54

Communication, as a regulatory mechanism of infant, 115

Concern and sympathy: expression of caregiver, 12; signal to maintain interaction, 12-13

Controlling behavior, caregiver's, 115-116

Coping mechanisms, infant's, 110-114

Curiosity, importance of, 54

Darwin, Charles, 42-43

Décarie, Therese G., 24

Discrepancy, source of stimulation and attention, 60

Doll-playing, 27

Education for caregiving: limitations and dangers of, 132; unique experiences of, 133

Eibl-Eibesfeldt, Irenaneus, 12, 25

Elicitation of caregiver's reaction. *See* Caregiver

Emde, Robert, 65

Engagement, episodes of, in play, 79-81; regular rate or tempo of, 80; limited variability in, 81;

DATE DUE

MAR 16 1998	
NOV 25 2001	
APR 20 2005	
GAYLORD	PRINTED IN U.S.A.